P9-CEO-734

TEAM BUILDING:
ISSUES AND ALTERNATIVES

Thomas E. Stenvig

TEAM BUILDING:
ISSUES AND ALTERNATIVES

WILLIAM G. DYER
Brigham Young University

ADDISON-WESLEY PUBLISHING COMPANY
Reading, Massachusetts • Menlo Park, California
London • Amsterdam • Don Mills, Ontario • Sydney

This book is in the Addison-Wesley series:

ORGANIZATION DEVELOPMENT

Editors:
Edgar H. Schein
Warren G. Bennis
Richard Beckhard

Copyright © 1977 by Addison-Wesley Publishing Company, Inc. Philippines copyright 1977 by Addison-Wesley Publishing Company, Inc.

All rights reserved. No part of this publication may be reproduced, stored in a retrieval system, or transmitted, in any form or by any means, electronic, mechanical photocopying, recording, or otherwise, without the prior written permission of the publisher. Printed in the United States of America. Published simultaneously in Canada. Library of Congress Catalog Card No. 77-076113.

ISBN: 0-201-01191-3
GHIJKLMNOP-DO-89876543

FOREWORD

It has been five years since the Addison-Wesley series on organization development published the books by Roeber, Galbraith, and Steele, and it is almost ten years since the series itself was launched in an effort to define the then-emerging field of organization development. Almost from its inception the series enjoyed a great success and helped to define what was then only a budding field of inquiry. Much has happened in the last ten years. There are now dozens of textbooks and readers on OD; research results are beginning to accumulate on what kinds of OD approaches have what effects; educational programs on planned change and OD are growing; and there are regional, national, and even international associations of practitioners of planned change and OD. All of these trends suggest that this area of practice has taken hold and found an important niche for itself in the applied social sciences and that its intellectual underpinnings are increasingly solidifying.

One of the most important trends we have observed in the last five years is the connecting of the field of planned change and OD to the mainstream of organization theory, organizational psychology, and organizational sociology. Although the field has its roots primarily in these underlying disciplines, it is only in recent years that basic textbooks in "organization behavior" have begun routinely referring to organization development as an applied area that students and managers alike must be aware of.

The editors of this series have attempted to keep an open mind on the question of when the series has fulfilled its function and should be allowed to die. The series should be kept alive only as long as new areas of knowledge and practice central to organization development are emerging. During the last year or so, several such areas have been defined, leading to the decision to continue the series.

On the applied side, it is clear that information is a basic nutrient for any kind of valid change process. Hence, a book on data gathering, surveys, and feedback methods is very timely. Nadler has done an especially important service in this area in focusing on the variety of methods which can be used in gathering information and feeding it back to clients. The book is eclectic in its approach, reflecting the fact that there are many ways to gather information, many kinds to be gathered, and many approaches to the feedback process to reflect the particular goals of the change program.

Team building and the appropriate use of groups continues to be a second key ingredient of most change programs. So far no single book in the field has dealt explicitly enough with this important process. Dyer's approach will help the manager to diagnose when to use and not use groups and, most important, how to carry out team building when that kind of intervention is appropriate.

One of the most important new developments in the area of planned change is the conceptualizing of how to work with large systems to initiate and sustain change over time. The key to this success is "transition management," a stage or process frequently referred to in change theories, but never explored systematically from both a theoretical and practical point of view. Beckhard and Harris present a model which will help the manager to think about this crucial area. In addition, they provide a set of diagnostic and action tools which will enable the change manager in large systems to get a concrete handle on transition management.

The area of organization design has grown in importance as organizations have become more complex. Davis and Lawrence provide a concise and definitive analysis of that particularly elusive organization design—the matrix organization—and elucidate clearly its forms, functions, and modes of operation.

Future volumes in the new series will explore the interconnections between OD and related areas which are becoming increasingly important to our total understanding of organizations, the process of management, and the nature of work. The whole quality-of-work-life area has spawned a growing concern with the nature of work itself and the context within which it occurs. Human-resource planning and career development are increasingly becoming organically linked to planned change programs. As people are discovering the variety of goals and aspirations which encompass different careers and life stages, more emphasis will have to be given to alternative work patterns and reward systems. All of these issues become even more complex in the multinational organization.

It is exciting to see our field develop, expand, strengthen its roots, and grow outward in many new directions. I believe that the core theory or the integrative framework is not yet at hand, but that the varied activities of the theoreticians, researchers, and practitioners of planned change and OD are increasingly relevant not only to the change manager, but also to line managers at all levels. As the recognition grows that part of *every* manager's job is to plan, initiate, and manage change, so will the relevance of concepts and methods in this area come to be seen as integral to the management process itself. It continues to be the goal of this series to provide such relevant concepts and methods to managers. I hope we have succeeded in some measure in this new series of books.

Cambridge, Massachusetts   Edgar H. Schein
June 1977

PREFACE

Over the past fifteen years, the role of the manager has changed significantly in many organizations. The strong manager capable of almost single-handedly turning around an organization or department, while still a folk hero in the eyes of many, has given way to the recent demands of increasingly complex systems for managers who are able to pull together people of diverse backgrounds, personalities, training, and experience and weld them into an effective working group.

This modern manager has shifted from dealing with problems on a one-on-one basis to solving more problems collectively, involving everyone that has a contribution to make in either solving a problem or implementing actions. In this context, the manager is a coach, a facilitator, a developer, a team builder. Many managers have not been trained in these new collaborative skills and this deficiency has given rise to the organization consultant, both external and internal, whose job it is to work with managers in developing a strong, viable working team.

This volume is written for both the manager and the consultant who are interested in knowing how to design and conduct a program in team development. The book begins with a case study of a manager who faces a range of commonly encountered problems, all involving the success or failure of a variety of organizational "teams" that make up his world. Following this is a review of the rise of the importance of teams in modern organizations and the methods developed for team building.

The next several chapters describe a wide range of alternative formats for dealing with the different kinds of problems that face work units. Those who are interested in conducting a team-development program should make a serious analysis of their own situation and then create a program specifically tailored to their needs. This is much more productive than applying a "canned" program that may prove inappropriate for the particular conditions that exist.

Team development is not a one-shot activity or a panacea for organizational problems. Rather, it is a long-range program for uniting people into shared efforts for improving the effectiveness of a working group.

I wish to acknowledge some of those who have contributed to the completion of this book. First, my family has been the laboratory for many of my attempts at team building. Many of my colleagues have stimulated my thinking in this field, particularly Jerry Harvey, Dick Beckhard, Jack Gibb, Bob Dyer, and Weldon Moffitt. I appreciate the editorial counsel of Ed Schein and the encouragement of Warren Bennis. Finally, I acknowledge my debt to those clients who have allowed me to work with them in team-building programs through the years.

Provo, Utah   W.G.D.
June 1977

CONTENTS

**PART 1
WHAT'S TEAM DEVELOPMENT ABOUT?**

1
TEAMS ARE EVERYWHERE

Jim Thomas is manager of the Mountain Side plant of the National Alloys Company. He has a tough production schedule that demands solid performance from all of his people, in all areas of the plant. Jim wants to do a top-flight job and becomes concerned when production drops, when problems go unsolved, or when morale sags.

After his job and his family, Jim's greatest interest is pro football—particularly as played by the Dallas Cowboys. Being a native Texan, Jim has followed the Dallas team from its inception. He gets to attend an occasional game and watches them regularly on TV or listens to them on the radio. When the game is over, Jim can give a clear, detailed accounting for the team's success or failure.

What raises Jim's boiling point higher than anything is to watch his team fail to play together. He can spot in an instant when someone misses a block, loafs on the job, fails to pass on obvious information to the quarterback, or tries to "shine" at the expense of the team. He can diagnose the Cowboys' areas of weakness, and, if the coach could only hear him, he would tell him what to do to remedy the situation. But with all of his insight about teamwork and football, Jim fails to see the parallels between what is needed to improve the Dallas Cowboys and what is needed to shape up the management team at National Alloys. Many of the problems are exactly the same:

1. Some individuals have never really learned what their assignment's are, particularly for certain plays or situations.

2. Some are afraid of the coach, so they pretend to know things that they should be asking questions about.

3. Some want to do things "the old way," while others feel that more modern methods are needed.

4. Factions and cliques quarrel and fight among one another.

5. The whole unit has not come together to develop common goals to which everyone is committed.

6. Decisions are made by someone, but some people either don't "get the word" or they disagree with the decision and drag their feet.

7. There is jealousy between units and a lack of playing together.

8. Even when people are aware of a problem, they don't know exactly what to do about it.

Teams are collections of people who must rely on group collaboration if each member is to experience the optimum of success and goal achievement. It is obvious that in order to score touchdowns (and prevent the opponent from scoring) a football team has to play together. It should be just as obvious that a work unit or a management group must also work together to ensure success. A football team practices over and over again how it will execute its plays. The team has "skull" practice—they talk over plans and strategies. They review films of past games, identify mistakes, set up goals for the next week. Unfortunately, Jim Thomas's management group does not engage in any similar type of activities. They do not review their past actions and they do not really plan new strategies. They do not come together to learn from their mistakes, nor do they practice or get coaching on new methods, set new goals, or build up their team "spirit." Jim Thomas can spot the absence of teamwork on the playing field, but cannot see similar symptoms in the work plant. He is aware that sometimes things are not running smoothly at work, but he is not sure just what is wrong and he does not know what he can do about it.

THE FAMILY TEAM

When Jim Thomas goes home at night, he enters into another "team," a most personal, sensitive, and important unit—his family. Here again is a group of people who must collaborate and combine resources in order that each group member may achieve his or her goals. Jim can easily feel those times when the right family spirit is missing. When his wife is upset or angry, when one of their children is troubled, or when Jim is tense and anxious, the entire family is affected. Morale droops. Here again, Jim is very sensitive to the interpersonal climate, but as in the work setting, he often feels helpless and inept when it comes to doing something about a problem situation.

OTHER TEAMS

If Jim would look more closely, he would be able to spot examples of human "teams" functioning either poorly or effectively all around him. At church, for example, Jim belongs to another team, the Planning and Finance Committee. He often is aware of long hours wasted in committee meetings because people are not prepared with reports that are needed, signals are not clear about assignments, decisions get "lost" and have to be made over again, or discussions bog down in fruitless arguments.

The community symphony orchestra that Jim's wife is chairman of is another team; like the Dallas Cowboys, they must practice and practice to ensure a coordinated performance. Even Jim, who is no great connoisseur of music, is aware when the orchestra is not playing together. At the last concert there was an embarrassing silence when the drums failed to sound at a critical moment.

Jim likes to go to his favorite gas station because everyone pitches in to give customers quick, efficient service. One attendant will take care of the gas and check under the hood, while the other cleans the windows and headlights. If anything needs changing, they bring it to Jim's attention, without high pressuring for a sale. The employees help each other without being asked. "A good team," Jim thinks.

Many people are like Jim—only vaguely aware that modern society is a complex of interdependent groups or teams. People are called on to work with each other in a variety of situations—work, home, school, clubs, church, and community and service organizations. Just like a football or basketball team, these organizational teams can malfunction and fail to score or win—and for many of the same reasons. All teams need good coaching or management. There needs to be review of past effort and rehearsal or replanning. Problems between members must be resolved; things that are unclear should be understood. Good teams stop and take stock of their performance, diagnose the problems, and then take actions to insure that at the time of the next game they are ready to play.

This book is about organizational teams—especially about what can be done to help a team diagnose problem areas and take actions to develop into a more effective working unit. Managers are like coaches. They must be able to look at the team effort with a practiced eye, see what is interfering with maximum effort (or find out what the blocks are), and then devise a strategy or plan to remove the obstacles and release people for maximum effort as they combine their resources to achieve common goals. That is the name of the game in team development.

Most managers are stopped from solving work unit problems either because they don't see what the real problems are or because they don't know exactly what to do. Hopefully this book will be helpful in overcoming both these obstacles, by providing a sound basis for making a correct diagnosis and by outlining team-building procedures that have proven to be effective.

2
EMERGENCE OF THE TEAM IDEA

One of the great breakthroughs in organization theory and practice came in the late 1920s and early 1930s with the now-classic Hawthorne Studies. This research, conducted by a group of Harvard professors at the Hawthorne, Illinois plant of the Western Electric Company, started out to test the hypothesis that work output is connected with work-area lighting or illumination. It was hypothesized that workers would work more efficiently under conditions of good lighting, an hypothesis that stemmed from the stimulus-response theory that individuals will respond directly to external stimuli and, if you can control the stimuli, you can control the individual effort.

The first phase of research resulted in some puzzling data. The experimental group's (those working under altered lighting) production output constantly increased, even though lighting decreased. This led to a series of research activities designed to examine in-depth what happens to a group of workers under various conditions. Six operators were selected to work in a special test group whose job it was to assemble telephone relays. Data were collected on this group for five years under a variety of conditions—rest periods and methods of pay were varied, refreshments and a shortened work week were tried, and so on. The researchers found that work output seemed to ultimately be a function of something more than rest periods, incentives, or refreshments. After much analysis, the researchers generally agreed that the most significant factor was the building of a sense of group identity, a feeling of social support and cohesion that came with increased worker interaction. Also, the superior or management leader was observed to behave somewhat differently toward the workers in the experimental group, and this, too, appeared to enhance the "team" spirit.

Elton Mayo, one of the original researchers, summarized the Hawthorne experiment this way:

These original provisions were effective largely because the experimental room was in charge of *an interested and sympathetic chief observer.* He understood clearly from the first that any hint of "the supervisor" in his methods might be fatal to the interests of the inquiry. So far as it was possible, he and his assistants kept the history sheets and the log sheet faithfully posted. In addition to this he *took a personal interest in each girl* and her achievement; *he showed pride in the record of the group.* He helped the group to feel that its duty was to *set its own conditions of work,* he helped the workers to find the "freedom" of which they so frequently speak.

In the early stages of development, it was inevitable that the group should become interested in its achievement and should to some extent enjoy the reflected glory of the interest the inquiry attracted. As the years passed this abated somewhat, but all the evidence—including the maintenance of a high output—goes to show that something in the reconditioning of the group must be regarded as a permanent achievement. At no time in the five-year period did the girls feel that they were working under pressure; on the contrary, they invariably cite the absence of this as their reason for preferring the "test room."

Undoubtedly, there had been a remarkable change of mental attitude in the group. This showed in their recurrent conferences with high executive authorities. At first shy and uneasy, silent and perhaps somewhat suspicious of the company's intention, later their attitude is marked by confidence and candor. *Before every change of program, the group is consulted.* Their comments are listened to and discussed; sometimes their objectives are allowed to negate a suggestion. *The group unquestionably develops a*

*sense of participation in the critical determinations and becomes
something of a social unit.*[1] (Italics added.)

The Hawthorne study illustrates some of the essential elements
that are important in team effectiveness, for the experiment showed
the possibility of taking a random collection of employees and building them into a highly productive work team. Mayo's discussion
above points out certain critical factors:

1. The boss (chief observer) had a personal interest in each person's
    achievement.

2. He took pride in the record of the group.

3. He helped the group work together to set its own conditions of
    work.

4. He faithfully posted the feedback on performance.

5. The group took pride in its own achievement and had the satisfac-
    tion of outsiders showing interest in what they did.

6. The group did not feel they were being pressured to change.

7. Before changes were made, the group was consulted.

8. The group developed a sense of confidence and candor.

These conditions for developing an effective work team, identified in a research effort begun in 1928, are still important considerations for managers nearly fifty years later.

RESEARCH ON GROUP BEHAVIOR

Since World War II, there has been a tremendous increase in the attention paid to the forces in groups that influence the actions of group
members. McGrath and Altman[2] did a snythesis and critique of the
small-group field in 1966, and their bibliography contains 2,699
entries. This research on group dynamics, group processes, and condi-

---

1   Elton Mayo, *The Human Problems of an Industrial Civilization* (Boston:
     Division of Research, Graduate School of Business Administration, Har-
     vard University, 1933). Quoted with permission.

2   J. E. McGrath and I. Altman, *Small Group Research* (New York: Holt,
     Rinehart and Winston, 1966).

tions has had considerable impact on the design of team-development programs. Such programs may now draw on a massive amount of research evidence. It is important that those planning team-development activities keep on top of the constant flow of new findings in the group-behavior field.

GROUP CONCEPTS IN MANAGEMENT

Two of the early writers in the area of management who began to emphasize the group-team concept as an important part of organization and management theory were Douglas McGregor and Rensis Likert. In the last chapter of *The Human Side of Enterprise,* McGregor discussed the managerial team. He describes a highly effective management team studied by researchers and notes the researchers' conclusion that "unity of purpose" was the main distinguishing characteristic of this successful unit.

> The significance of unity of purpose within a managerial team is given some lip service by most managers, but it is not always recognized that this objective can only be achieved by a closely knit *group.* Most so-called managerial teams are not teams at all, but collections of individual relationships with the boss in which each individual is vying with every other for power, prestige, recognition, and personal autonomy. Under such conditions unity of purpose is a myth.
>
> One research study of top management groups found that 85 percent of the communications within the group took place between individual subordinates and the superior (up *and* down), and only 15 percent laterally between the subordinates. Many executives who talk about their "teams" of subordinates would be appalled to discover how low is the actual level of collaboration among them, and how high is the mutual suspicion and antagonism. Yet these same executives generally create the very conditions which would appall them if recognized. They do so by managing individuals rather than helping to create a genuine group.[3]

3   Douglas McGregor, *The Human Side of Enterprise* (New York: McGraw-Hill, 1960), pp. 228–229.

At the time McGregor was writing, William W. Whyte had just written a book, *Organization Man,* in which he decried the use of groups in organizations, claiming that group activities had a depressing or leveling effect on individual performance and stultified creativity and individual expression. McGregor commented:

> These views [of Whyte] deny the realities of organizational life. Many activities simply cannot be carried on and many problems cannot be solved on an individual basis or in two person relationships. . . .
>
> In general we are remarkably inept in accomplishing objectives through group effort. This is not inevitable. It is a result of inadequate understanding and skill with respect to the unique aspects of group operation.
>
> Whyte's thesis that we have given undue emphasis to group phenomena, and in the process lost track of individuals, misses the point altogether. The real problem is that we have given so little attention to group behavior that management does not know enough about how to create the conditions for individual growth and integrity in the group situation. The problem is one of ignorance based on under, not overemphasis.[4]

McGregor then identified the characteristics of an effective work team (see Fig. 2.1).

At the same time McGregor's book was having its impact, Likert, in *New Patterns of Management*, was developing his notion of organizations as a series of interlocking groups and the manager as a "linking pin." As he studied the research literature, Likert felt that managers must learn to cope with a totality of people under their direction and not just manage individuals one-on-one. Likert's "ideal" form of management (System 4) is called "Participative Group" management.[5] Likert identified twenty-four properties and performance characteristics of the ideal, highly effective group, as noted in Fig. 2.2.

---

4   Ibid., pp. 229–230.
5   Rensis Likert, *New Patterns of Management* (New York: McGraw-Hill, 1961).

Fig. 2.1   McGregor's characteristics of an effective work team. (From Douglas McGregor, *The Human Side of Enterprise,* pp. 232–235. Copyright © 1960. Used with permission of McGraw-Hill Book Company.)

1. The "atmosphere" tends to be informal, comfortable, relaxed. There are no obvious tensions. It is a working atmosphere in which people are involved and interested. There are no signs of boredom.

2. There is a lot of discussion in which virtually everyone participates, but it remains pertinent to the task of the group. If the discussion gets off the subject, someone will bring it back in short order.

3. The task or the objective of the group is well understood and accepted by the members. There will have been free discussion of the objective at some point, until it was formulated in such a way that the members of the group could commit themselves to it.

4. The members listen to each other! The discussion does not have the quality of jumping from one idea to another unrelated one. Every idea is given a hearing. People do not appear to be afraid of being foolish by putting forth a creative thought even if it seems fairly extreme.

5. There is disagreement. The group is comfortable with this and shows no signs of having to avoid conflict or to keep everything on a plane of sweetness and light. Disagreements are not suppressed or overridden by premature group action. The reasons are carefully examined, and the group seeks to resolve them rather than to dominate the dissenter.

   On the other hand, there is no "tyranny of the minority." Individuals who disagree do not appear to be trying to dominate the group or to express hostility. Their disagreement is an expression of a genuine difference of opinion, and they expect a hearing in order that a solution may be found.

   Sometimes there are basic disagreements which cannot be resolved. The group finds it possible to live with them, accepting them but not permitting them to block its efforts. Under some conditions, action will be deferred to permit further study of an issue between the members. On other occasions, where the disagreement cannot be resolved and action is necessary, it will be taken but with open caution and recognition that the action may be subject to later reconsideration.

6. Most decisions are reached by a kind of consensus in which it is clear that everybody is in general agreement and willing to go along. However, there is little tendency for individuals who oppose the action to keep their opposition private and thus let an apparent consensus mask real disagreement. Formal voting is at a minimum; the group does not accept a simple majority as a proper basis for action.

7. Criticism is frequent, frank, and relatively comfortable. There is little evidence of personal attack, either openly or in a hidden fashion. The criticism has a constructive flavor in that it is oriented toward removing an obstacle that faces the group and prevents it from getting the job done.

8. People are free in expressing their feelings as well as their ideas both on the problem and on the group's operation. There is little pussyfooting, there are few "hidden agendas." Everybody appears to know quite well how everybody else feels about any matter under discussion.

9. When action is taken, clear assignments are made and accepted.

10. The chairman of the group does not dominate it, nor on the contrary, does the group defer unduly to him or her. In fact, as one observes the activity, it is clear that the leadership shifts from time to time, depending on the circumstances. Different members, because of their knowledge or experience, are in a position at various times to act as "resources" for the group. The members utilize them in this fashion and they occupy leadership roles while they are thus being used. There is little evidence of a struggle for power as the group operates. The issue is not who controls, but how to get the job done.

11. The group is self-conscious about its own operations. Frequently, it will stop to examine how well it is doing or what may be interfering with its operation. The problem may be a matter or procedure, or it may be an individual whose behavior is interfering with the accomplishment of the group's objectives. Whatever it is, it gets open discussion until a solution is found.

Fig. 2.2 Likert's characteristics of an effective work group. (From Rensis Likert, *New Patterns of Management,* pp. 166–169. Copyright © 1961. Used with permission of McGraw-Hill Book Company.)

1. Members are skilled in all the various leadership and membership roles and functions required for interaction between leaders and members and between members and other members.

2. The group has been in existence sufficiently long to have developed a well-established, relaxed working relationship among all its members.

3. The members of the group are attracted to it and are loyal to its members, including the leader.

4. The members and leaders have a high degree of confidence and trust in each other.

5. The values and goals of the group are a satisfactory integration and expression of the relevant values and needs of its members. They have helped shape these values and goals and are satisfied with them.

6. Insofar as members of the group are performing linking functions, they endeavor to have the values and goals of the groups which they link in harmony, one with the other.

7. The more important a value seems to the group, the greater the likelihood that the individual member will accept it.

8. The members of the group are highly motivated to abide by the major values and to achieve the important goals of the group. Each member will do all that he or she reasonably can—and at times all in his or her power—to help the group achieve its central objectives. Each member expects every other member to do the same.

9. All the interaction, problem-solving, decision-making activities of the group occur in a supportive atmosphere. Suggestions, comments, ideas, information, criticisms are all offered with a helpful orientation. Similarly, these contributions are received in the same spirit. Respect is shown for the point of view of others both in the way contributions are made and in the way they are received.

10. The superior of each work group exerts a major influence in establishing the tone and atmosphere of that work group by his or her leadership principles and practices. In the highly effective group, consequently, the leader adheres to those principles of leadership which create a supportive atmosphere in the group and a cooperative rather than a competitive relationship among the members.

11. The group is eager to help each member develop to his or her full potential. It sees, for example, that relevant technical knowledge and training in interpersonal and group skills are made available to each member.

12. Each member accepts willingly and without resentment the goals and expectations that the individual and the group establish for themselves. The anxieties, fears, and emotional stresses produced by direct pressure for high performance from a boss in a hierarchical situation are not present. Groups seem capable of setting high performance goals for the group as a whole and for each member. These goals are high enough to stimulate each member to do his or her best, but not so high as to create anxieties or fear of failure. In an effective group, each person can exert sufficient influence on the decisions of the group to prevent the group from setting unattainable goals for any member while setting high goals for all. The goals are adapted to the member's capacity to perform.

13. The leader and the members believe that each group member can accomplish the "impossible." These expectations stretch each member to the maximum and accelerate personal growth. When necessary, the group tempers the expectation level so that the member is not broken by a feeling of failure or rejection.

14. When necessary or advisable, other members of the group will give a member the help needed to accomplish successfully the goals set for that person. Mutual help is a characteristic of highly effective groups.

15. The supportive atmosphere of the highly effective group stimulates creativity. The group does not demand narrow conformity as do the work groups under authoritarian leaders. No one has to "yes the boss," nor is a person rewarded for such an attempt.

(continued)

The group attaches high value to new, creative approaches and solutions to its problems and to the problems of the organization of which it is a part.

16. The group knows the value of "constructive" conformity and knows when to use it and for what purposes. Although it does not permit conformity to affect adversely the creative efforts of its members, it does expect conformity on mechanical and administrative matters to save the time of members and to facilitate the group's activities.

17. There is strong motivation on the part of each member to communicate fully and frankly to the group all the information which is relevant and of value to the group's activity.

18. There is high motivation in the group to use the communication process so that it best serves the interests and goals of the group. Every item which a member feels is important, but which for some reason is being ignored, will be repeated until it receives the attention that it deserves. Members strive also to avoid communicating unimportant information so as not to waste the group's time.

19. Just as there is high motivation to communicate, there is correspondingly strong motivation to receive communications. Each member is genuinely interested in any information on any relevant matter that any member of the group can provide. This information is welcomed and trusted as being honestly and sincerely given. Members do not look "behind" information and attempt to interpret it in ways opposite to its purported intent.

20. In the highly effective group, there are strong motivations to try to influence other members as well as to be receptive to influence by them. This applies to all the group's activities: technical matters, methods, organizational problems, interpersonal relationships, and group processes.

21. The group processes of the highly effective group enable the members to exert more influence on the leader and to communicate far more information to him or her, including suggestions as to what needs to be done and how the leader could do a better job, than is possible in a one-to-one relationship. By "tossing the

ball" back and forth among the members, a group can communicate information to the leader which no single person on a one-to-one basis dare do.

22. The ability of the members of a group to influence each other contributes to the flexibility and adaptability of the group. Ideas, goals, and attitudes do not become frozen if members are able to influence each other continuously.

23. In the highly effective group, individual members feel secure in making decisions which seem appropriate to them because the goals and philosophy of operation are clearly understood by each member and provide a solid base for making decisions. This unleashes initiative and pushes decisions down while still maintaining a coordinated and directed effort.

24. The leader of a highly effective group is selected carefully. His or her leadership ability is so evident that he or she would probably emerge as a leader in any unstructured situation. To increase the likelihood that persons of high leadership competence are selected, the organization is likely to use peer nominations and related methods in selecting group leaders.

Blake and Mouton have widely used the team analogy in describing their "9, 9 management":

Because the word team is likely to be used to refer to any set of individuals who cooperate in accomplishing a single overall result, the question can be asked whether team action of the kind being described leads to conformity pressures which dampen individuality and stifle independence of effort. The answer is that the opposite is true. True team action is more like a football situation where division of effort is meshed into a single coordinated result; where the whole is more, and different, than the sum of its individual parts. Here, there is a common set of signals, based on understanding, which dictate action—a division of closely knitted individual activity combined with interdependent effort is the 9,9 pattern of integrating individual with organizational effort.[6]

6   Robert Blake and Jane Mouton, *The Managerial Grid* (Houston: Gulf Publishing Co., 1964).

They point out that a good team has task specialization and division of labor.

> Each person shoulders a different part of the total job, with each having 100 percent responsibility for success of the whole. . . . Furthermore, it has in common a set of strategies to fit a variety of situations and signals which are well understood . . . and includes:
>
> 1.   Team action based on synchronized effort of all.
>
> 2.   Pair action, i.e., based on meshing of effort between coach-quarterback, quarterback-center, etc.
>
> 3.   Solo effort, i.e., broken field running, pass interception, etc.[7]

How do you go about training managers to manage teams? Blake and Mouton state:

> The question becomes, How do organizations which recognize the importance of team action go about training to get it?
>
> A simple answer can be given by analogy to a baseball or football team. Both of these are organizations in a very real sense, and both are concerned with team action. Ridiculous though it sounds, if the conventional approach of training individuals one-by-one were applied in developing a baseball or a football team, each of the team members would be trained at the hands of specialists, also one-by-one, away from the organization and isolated from the others with whom he must eventually engage in team action. Then, all members would be returned to the organization and thrown together on the assumption that since all had learned individually, they automatically would be able to work together effectively. There would literally be no need for practice, and no one would think to help the team develop a set of common signals, because each person should have learned all that he needed to learn in his own specialized training program in order to become an effective team member.
>
> The absurdity of this can further be seen in the analogy of the football team where each designated individual would gain specialized training in schools, one school concerned with training guards, another with centers, etc. After persons had been trained

---

individually, they would be returned to the football club for the purpose of playing together in the belief that an effective team operation would result after skills of individuals had been perfected. Both of these examples point to the fallacy in logic of a conventional approach to training when the goal of organizational health is successful team action.[8]

RECENT TRENDS

Since these early references to the importance of teams in work systems, the demand for more effective work units has increased and more recent writers have explored new developments in organization theory and practice.

One of the current trends in many modern organizations is to move towards a matrix or program structure.[9] In this type of system, a new work group is created by drawing on people from several functional departments. For example, a new project, program or product group may be developed by pulling together needed people from such existing departments as marketing, research and development, sales, production, engineering, finance, and personnel. The function of this new unit is to develop a new product or program. Members of the unit belong to two groups—the basic functional department and the new program or product group. In these situations, an employee can feel fractured, split, or isolated in work relations unless the managers of both units to which the employee has membership know how to create an environment where the person feels involved and committed. Team development is important to build the new program group rapidly and to maintain the person's identity with his or her functional unit.

Lawrence and Lorsch[10] have made a strong case for their "differentiation-integration" model of organizations. According to this analysis, it is important that different departments in organizations

---

8   R.R. Blake, J.S. Mouton, and M.G. Blansfield, "How Executive Team Training Can Help You." Reproduced by special permission from the January 1962 *Training and Development Journal.* Copyright 1962 by the American Society for Training and Development, Inc.

9   For a discussion of the matrix organization see Jay Galbraith, *Designing Complex Organizations* (Reading, Mass.: Addison-Wesley, 1973), Chapter 7.

10   Paul Lawrence and Jay Lorsch, *Organization and Environment: Managing Differentiation and Integration* (Boston: Harvard Graduate School of Business Administration, Division of Research, 1967).

develop along differential lines. A sales department should be, and usually is, different in its organization and functioning from a manufacturing group. They have differing kinds of tasks, people, goals, and time limits. It would be unwise to demand that all departments follow a single model of organization and functioning. This means that team-development programs will vary with the needs of the differing departments. Lawrence and Lorsch also make the strong point that, with work units that may be highly differentiated, it is important for purposes of common goal setting, planning, and coordination to work out an effective method of integration—tying the groups together. One of the widely used integrating mechanisms is the coordinating or integrating team. Members of this group must represent their own departments as well as work out common issues with the other units. In such a situation, team development of the integrating group may become a high priority item in an organization development program.

The fields of group dynamics and laboratory education have contributed much toward building a theory and method for using groups as a basis of organization change. Schein and Bennis[11] have carefully outlined procedures for using the group to successfully introduce changes both at the individual and organizational level. Bradford, Gibb, and Benne[12] wrote the basic volume on the methods of laboratory education and Luft[13] developed a group communication model (The Johari Window), which is another way of thinking of effective group interaction. All of these orientations have emphasized the importance of the human group as a basis of integrating people into organizations and using group methods for building effective work relationships. Team building, as we explore it in this book, is an outgrowth of all of these constructs and methods.

11   Edgar H. Schein and Warren G. Bennis, *Personal and Organizational Change Through Group Methods* (New York: Wiley, 1965).

12   Leland P. Bradford, Jack R. Gibb, and Kenneth D. Benne, *T-Group Theory and Laboratory Method* (New York: Wiley, 1964).

13   Joseph Luft, *Of Human Interaction* (Palo Alto: National Press Books, 1969).

3
METHODS IN TEAM DEVELOPMENT

With the emergence of the idea that organizations are composed of interlocking work groups or teams came also the methods for building more effective work teams.

A BLENDING OF THEORY AND METHOD

The methodology of "team development" in organizations grew out of the historical blending of a theory and a method. During the late 1950s and early 1960s, the thrust of management theory centered on the works of McGregor, Likert, and Blake and Mouton, as has been noted. All of these writers began to emphasize the apparent advantages of participative management over more traditional authoritarian approaches. Managers who were exposed to these authors and saw themselves as Theory X; or 1,1; or System 1, began to ask, "How can I change myself and my organization in the direction of Theory Y; 9,9; or System 4?"

The methodology that was available at the time to help in that transformation was the training group, variously called the T-group, sensitivity group, encounter group, or basic group. The purposes of such group training were to help participants examine group processes, experience group problem solving, openly share information, establish a highly cohesive group climate, and build norms of shared and collaborative action. These group-centered processes, developed usually in groups of strangers with a strong focus on the examination of "here and now" activity, resulted in a sharing of a good deal of feedback as to how group members experienced each other.

PROBLEMS IN THE "FAMILY" GROUP

The T-group methodology was transferred into the organizational setting as the most effective method practitioners knew at the time for: (1) implementing the ideas of participative management, and (2) changing a work unit from System 1 or Theory X to System 4 or Theory Y. Unfortunately, the T-group method that was so successful in stranger groups had mixed results when used with "family" groups—groups composed of persons who had worked together for years in the same department. Some of the major problems that occurred were: (1) The T-group with strangers assumed a vacuum of past experience; hence, the focus on what was happening right now was most appropriate. Work groups had a long history of associations and activities. T-group trainers were not sure what areas to explore and what to leave alone. (2) T-groups disbanded and never met again while the work unit continued intact after the sessions and people had to be responsible through time for issues raised in the group.

Harvey and Davis[1] identify additionally nine other differences between the T-group in a laboratory organization and the nonlaboratory or work unit.

1. Participants in laboratories are similar in personality structure. Their value systems are essentially congruent with the values of laboratory training and laboratory trainers. Persons from nonlaboratory organizations tend to have much more diverse, or at least different, personality structures.

2. Laboratories are temporary systems. Nonlaboratory organizations tend to have continuity and long-term existence.

---

1   Jerry B. Harvey and Sheldon A. Davis, "Some Differences between Laboratory and Non-Laboratory Organizations," in W. G. Dyer, ed., *Modern Theory and Method in Group Training* (New York: Van Nostrand Reinhold, 1972).

3. In the laboratory, the problem is to build an organization. In other organizations, the problem usually is to change existing organizational systems.

4. Laboratories are social systems. Nonlaboratory organizations are sociotechnical systems.

5. Laboratories are oriented toward the individual and small groups. Nonlaboratory units are oriented toward the larger organization.

6. Laboratory trainers are line managers. Organization consultants are staff persons.

7. Laboratory organizations provide rewards which are essentially intrinsic in character. Nonlaboratory organizations tend to provide rewards which are extrinsic.

8. Data are more readily available in laboratory organizations than in nonlaboratory organizations.

9. Feedback is more readily available and less equivocal in laboratory than in nonlaboratory organizations.

As practitioners developed more experience in applying the T-group methods to work units, the T-group mode shifted to take into account the differences of the new setting. It became clear that the need was not just to let people get feedback, but to help the work unit develop into a more effective, collaborative, problem-solving unit with work to get out and goals to achieve. Slowly the methodology shifted from the unstructured T-group to a more focused, defined process of training a group of interdependent people in collaborative work and problem-solving procedures.

THE CASE FOR TEAM DEVELOPMENT

Managers in organizations have for years engaged in management training or development. It has become commonplace for managers to go away to various training programs in hopes of returning with new insights or skills that would improve their own and others' effectiveness. Unfortunately, the evidence from research has not indicated that sending people away results in major improvements in the back-home

setting. It has been noted that when a manager returns to the work setting, the unit to which he or she belongs continues in the old behavior,
and, eventually, the pressures and influences of the back-home situation erase the effect of the training. This has led managers to re-
examine the type of training they feel would result in change. Team
development suggests that the unit in need of training or change is *not*
the individual manager, but the whole working group. Everyone who
works together needs to learn new, more effective ways of problem
solving, planning, decision making, coordination, integrating resources, sharing information, and dealing with problem situations
that arise. If the total unit can be changed, there is strong likelihood
that new behavior will be maintained through time.

Galbraith[2] makes a strong case that team development is a viable
alternative in redesigning organizations. If an organization is experi-
encing work overload, decision-making difficulties, problems in
lateral relationships, or problems in information flow and scheduling,
there are a variety of redesign possibilities, but creating new teams or
task forces or building up poor performing units is certainly an important method in improving the organization.

Team-building activities began to increase rapidly during the
latter part of the 1960s and early 1970s. Many managers pushed to
have team-development programs introduced into their organizations
without critically analyzing whether or not this methodology was
appropriate for their situation. In the next chapter, we consider how
to determine if a team-development program would be useful in an
organization seeking change.

---

2   Jay Galbraith, *Designing Complex Organizations* (Reading, Mass.:
    Addison-Wesley, 1973), Chapter 6.

PART 2
IMPLEMENTING TEAM DEVELOPMENT

4
IS A TEAM-DEVELOPMENT PROGRAM NEEDED?

Before any organizational unit begins a team-development program, a systematic assessment as to the conditions that need improvement and the appropriateness of team building as the change method is essential. Following are two actual cases concerning the decision to begin a change program using team development.

CASE A: THE HLW DEPARTMENT

The HLW department is an agency of a state government. It has a central office in the capital city and a series of district offices throughout the state. The agency employs about 500 people and is headed by an executive director who has twelve different department heads reporting to her. Through the years, the agency has been seen by other similar agencies and by the people in the department as doing an effective job in spite of difficult circumstances.

The decision regarding some type of training or development was faced initially by the training and development officer and his assistant. They were reviewing their training budget and were very much aware that approximately $5,000 of unexpended funds remained in the year's budget with less than six months to go. They also knew the training budget might be cut if unused funds were returned to the general fund, and that questions would be raised about

27

the effectiveness of the training department if funds that were allocated, presumably against a preplanned program, were not used.

The two training and development staff people considered several alternatives. First, they rejected the returning of unspent funds. This left them with the alternative of spending the funds. But what type of expenditure would make sense and make a contribution to the department? The assistant commented, "I recently read a good article on organization development. In my opinion, we need some OD work done in our agency."

The training director replied, "That sounds good to me, but how do you get OD started in an organization?"

"From what I read, one of the best ways is to do some team building."

"What's that?" asked the director.

"My understanding is that people who have to work together should learn how to communicate and to solve their problems so they stay solved," said the assistant. "And that sounds to me like something our executive committee [the executive director and the twelve department heads] could really use."

"You can say that again," responded the training director. "But how can we sell that group on a team-building program?"

The assistant thought for a moment. "I think they would go for this program if we could get a good outside consultant to come in and conduct the program for the executive committee. An outside person would be a strong selling point to the committee."

"Agreed," said the T.D. "Let's see if we can line up a good outside person. You get a reprint of that article on OD and we'll circulate that to the executive committee. If we can get the consultant and can set up a time and place for the team-development program that suits everyone, I think we will be in business."

For the next few weeks the training director and his assistant were extremely busy. They contacted several people who were recommended as effective leaders of team-development programs. At least two would be available during the most likely times. The OD article was circulated to all relevant people and a meeting was set up with the executive director. They reviewed the plans with the director.

Her response was favorable. "It all looks pretty good. I think we should go ahead. My own schedule is very tight and I may not be able to stay the whole time, but I can be there to start it out and then I may have to duck out to attend some meetings in Washington. If you have a good outside person, I'm sure the whole thing will move along."

"That's my feeling," said the training director. "A good consultant will make a big difference."

So the plans were developed. A consultant was hired who had impressive credentials and his resume was circulated to the committee. An attractive resort was scheduled for three days. The consultant indicated that he would like to interview people for a couple of days prior to the program and that was agreed on. The executive director raised the team-development issue with the committee. Several people commented that they were "awfully busy," but the executive director was able to overcome these objections by pointing out that "certainly no one could disagree that it was critically important that this group become as effective a team as possible." With that, the motion to move ahead with the team-development program was unanimously approved.

CASE B: THE R & D DEPARTMENT

Tom Haymond, manager of the research and development department of the chemicals division of a large manufacturing company, had just returned from a management training program. It had been an intensive five days and he had heard some things about his own management style and strategy that bothered him. Tom knew things were not going all that well in his department. Because of that, he had contacted the training office and asked them to recommend a good management development course—maybe he could get some new ideas that would be helpful. The training office had directed him to a well-known program that had a strong laboratory-training-group focus and Tom made arrangements to attend.

The week's activity had been a real eye-opener for Tom. The seven other people in his group had given him a lot of feedback about the way he tried to handle things in the group, and there were a lot of comments when he described how he ran his department back home. Tom knew he was a hard-driving, results-oriented person; he couldn't stand to see anyone or anything just sitting around. The group members at the conference told him that his insistence that the group get organized and moving had really antagonized them, and some had deliberately tried to block his efforts. One member commented that she would certainly not like to work under Tom, if Tom were the same way back home as he was when the group started. Tom was quite sure he was the same way back home. That's what bothered him.

Tom had talked with his group facilitator before he left and got an agreement that if Tom wanted to do something in his own department, the facilitator would be available to help as an outside resource person.

After returning home from the conference, Tom spent part of several days planning a strategy. Finally he was ready to take action. He called an extended staff meeting for all of the section heads and project directors who reported to him—a group of ten people. At the staff meeting, Tom laid out a series of issues and concerns:

1. He described the conditions in the department that had led him to attend the training course—the number of new developments was down, some key people had recently quit or asked for transfers, in one exit interview the terminating person had placed the reason for leaving on Tom's ineffective management behavior, and the attendance and participation at staff meetings was low.

2. Tom summarized the feedback given him at the management program. He pointed out his concern about the feedback and his fear that his behavior at work was similar to that displayed during the conference. He felt that if he were to get feedback from the work group, it would be similar.

3. Tom then pointed out the dilemma for him. On the one hand he wanted to improve the performance level of the R & D department, but, on the other hand, he had some information that indicated he himself might be a contributing factor to low performance. Without clear feedback both from them to him and from him to them, they might not get the basic problems. A plan of action for improving the situation was badly needed.

4. Tom asked for their suggestions. "What can I do and what can you do to help us all work on the problems that I have identified?" There was a long silence. One project head said, "I don't think things are as bad as you paint them Tom. In my book, you're a pretty good manager." (There were nods of agreement and someone said, "Right on!")

Tom replied, "I appreciate your support, but I think we would all have to agree that this department has not been as effective recently as it was two years ago. Something has happened and I'd like to find out what that is and remedy it.

"I would like to make a suggestion. I propose that we spend two or three days away from the office looking intensively at the issues I have raised today. Each person would then come prepared to give his or her own information—what basic problems affect each of us personally on the job, what causes these problems, and what we might do about them. If we put all of our information together, we might come up with some interesting new solutions.

"Also, I would like to recommend bringing in an outside resource person to help us during the two-to-three-day meeting. This person could watch us work and see if anything in my actions or the way we work together might need improving. What do you think?"

The staff began to discuss the proposal at length and, after an intensive wrestling with the issues presented, the group agreed both to go ahead with the meeting (it would start Wednesday evening and finish Friday afternoon) and to bring in an outside resource person.

CASE A AND CASE B CONSIDERED

When we examine these two cases, it is obvious that the motivations for beginning a team-development program are quite different for the two organizations. The HLW Department needs to maintain its budget and its image. There is low commitment on the part of the executive director, but she uses her influence to "sell" the program to the executive committee. They all go along, but one could predict that when the executive director leaves after the first day, the level of effective action taking will drop even lower. Also, the outside consultant has inadvertently allowed his reputation to be the selling point for the program. There is little commitment on the part of anyone towards really working on team-development needs; in fact, the data suggest that the people are generally satisfied with the current performance. One would predict—accurately as it turned out—that the team-development program would have little chance for making any real difference in how that group works together.

Case B is quite different. Most of the elements necessary for beginning a positive team-development program are present. The manager has a high level of commitment to the program. He has involved his staff members early in the problem and enlisted their participation in the decision to go ahead. The boss has some insights already about his possible role in lower performance. This prepares him for negative information that may come—it will not be such a shock for people to present sensitive data or for him to hear it. The role of the outside person has been identified. The burden of the program is not on the consultant; rather, the main action is with the team. The resource person is an outside helper, not the one directing the effort. Again, it could be expected that the program would have a good chance of leading to some action steps that make a difference, and, in fact, it did.

ASSESSING THE ORGANIZATION'S NEED FOR TEAM DEVELOPMENT

Team development should begin with a strong "felt need" to improve some basic condition or process that is interfering with the achievement of organizational goals.

An organization, simply defined, is the arrangement and utlization of resources (human, financial, and material) for the accomplishment of goals. Sometime in the life of almost all organizations comes a point when members of the system are faced with two disturbing conditions that demand some pressure for change. One of these involves organizational consequences or *outputs,* and the other involves organizational *processes* or *dynamics.* When either of these begins to falter, change considerations and strategies come into focus. It is important to observe these conditions as a way of making an initial diagnosis as to the need of a team-building effort.

Organizational Outputs

All organizations, by definition, are goal oriented. When these goals, which are the ultimate achievement or output of the system, are not achieved to an adequate or satisfying degree, concern for change emerges. In our current economic system, all businesses are profit oriented. When the profit margin falls below a certain level defined as adequate, pressures for change are going to result. If profits are related to attendant conditions, such as production, sales, quality, service, labor turnover, markets, etc., then possible changes in these conditions are going to be examined. In Case B described above, there is some evidence that the amount of new suggestions, products, and developments has declined over the past two years in the R & D department. This has led Haymond to want to begin some action, even though he is not sure of the cause of the lower productivity.

If the organization is service oriented, such as a school, church, hospital, or government agency, and the level of customer utilization of service drops below some desired level, then someone begins to plan for change. No organization can (or perhaps even should) continue to exist if it cannot maintain itself at some adequate level of organizational output or goal achievement. Pressures to change something emerge with failing outputs, and it is generally the function of management to plan and take some action to minimize or reverse these negative or undesired outputs. A critical part of any manager's job is to plan a strategy that will be effective in reversing negative outputs. The organization in Case A is a service organization, but there is no indication that the outputs of the agency have fallen below the level of management satisfaction. There is little felt need to engage in a change program.

Organizational Processes

Within every organization, there is also some standard of acceptable process, dynamics, or means by which the organization's outputs are achieved. When conditions drop below this standard, be it a formal or informal one, managers also begin to plan for change. Concern for change stems from two sources: (1) if processes drop too low, the organizational outputs may be affected; and (2) if processes are too disrupted, the organization as a medium of human activity becomes too dissatisfying and the desire to improve the quality of life prompts change.

Almost no one enjoys working in a system where employees are subjected to constant criticism, isolation, conflict, alienation, over-control, low need satisfaction, and feelings of futility and frustration. It is unlikely that any organization beset with these conditions could maintain its outputs over the long haul, but even disregarding the outputs, most modern managers would feel a responsibility for improving the general life quality of human beings in the system. Tom Haymond has been given some feedback that suggests to him that he may be overcontrolling the work life of people under him. This leads him to want to check this possibility out with his people and to find out how they experience his managerial behavior.

If the standard of acceptable processes has been objectified, then grievance rates, turnover rates, absenteeism, complaints, transfer requests, and early retirements function as indicators that something in the organizational dynamics and processes is not functioning adequately—and, again, someone in management needs to plan some changes somewhere. Even where objective measures are not used, most managers are sensitive to climate factors, conflicts, hostilities, or disruptions that occur in their departments, and these, too, signal that something needs to be done to improve conditions. While the R & D division has both output and process problems, the state agency appears content at both levels.

PROBLEM IDENTIFICATION

Usually a team-building program will begin when the manager becomes aware of a certain concern, problem, issue, or set of symptoms that leads him or her to believe that the effectiveness of the staff or work unit is not at an appropriate level. Below is a list of major symptoms or conditions that usually would bring a manager to the point of seriously thinking about some remedial actions.

Symptoms that might signal the need for a team-building program include:

1. loss of production or unit output;

2. increase of grievances or complaints within the staff;

3. evidence of conflicts or hostility among staff members;

4. confusion about assignments, missed signals, and unclear relationships;

5. decisions misunderstood or not carried through properly;

6. apathy and general lack of interest or involvement of staff members;

7. lack of initiation, imagination, innovation—routine actions taken for solving complex problems;

8. ineffective staff meetings, low participation, minimal effective decisions;

9. start up of a new group that needs to develop quickly into a working team;

10. high dependency or negative reactions to the manager;

11. complaints from users or customers about quality of service;

12. continued unaccounted increase of costs.

Usually it is the manager who identifies one or more of the above conditions, although any unit member may share personal observations and diagnosis. Fig. 4.1 presents a checklist for identifying whether or not a team-development program is needed and whether the organization is ready to begin such a program. In Case B, we can see that Haymond is aware of several of these conditions in his own department. This awareness triggers off the change action.

TEAM DEVELOPMENT AS A CHANGE STRATEGY

When a unit of human beings joined together to reach goals finds that it no longer has the capability to really solve its problems well or reach its goals at an acceptable level, it may need to look for a way to reshape itself.

Team development is one process for revitalizing a social system. When the diagnosis that results from adequate data gathering indicates that the work unit no longer is functioning productively, a team-development program may be advisable as a strategy to improve effectiveness. In Case B above, Tom Haymond has enough initial data to go to his work group and suggest a team-development program.

The underlying reason for starting a team-development program is an important factor to consider. A program should not begin unless there is clear evidence that a lack of effective teamwork is the fundamental problem. If the problem is an intergroup issue, a technical difficulty, or an administrative foul-up, team building would not be an appropriate change strategy.

Fig. 4.1 Team-building checklist

I. Problem identification: To what extent is there evidence of the following problems in your work unit?

	Low evidence		Some evidence		High evidence
1. Loss of production or work-unit output.	1	2	3	4	5
2. Grievances or complaints within the work unit.	1	2	3	4	5
3. Conflicts or hostility between unit members.	1	2	3	4	5
4. Confusion about assignments or unclear relationships between people	1	2	3	4	5
5. Lack of clear goals, or low commitment to goals.	1	2	3	4	5
6. Apathy or general lack of interest or involvement of unit members.	1	2	3	4	5
7. Lack of innovation, risk taking, imagination, or taking initiative.	1	2	3	4	5
8. Ineffective staff meetings.	1	2	3	4	5
9. Problems in working with the boss.	1	2	3	4	5
10. Poor communications: people afraid to speak up, not listening to each other, or not talking together.	1	2	3	4	5
11. Lack of trust between boss and member or between members.	1	2	3	4	5
12. Decisions made that people do not understand or agree with.	1	2	3	4	5
13. People feel that good work is not recognized or rewarded.	1	2	3	4	5

	Low evidence		Some evidence		High evidence
14. People are not encouraged to work together in better team effort.	1	2	3	4	5

Scoring: Add up the score for the fourteen items. If your score is between 14–28, there is little evidence your unit needs team building. If your score is between 29–42, there is some evidence, but no immediate pressure, unless two or three items are very high. If your score is between 43–56, you should seriously think about planning the team-building program. If your score is over 56, then building should be a top priority item for your work unit.

II. Are you (or your manager) prepared to start a team-building program? Consider the following statements. To what extent do they apply to you or your department?

	Low		Medium		High
1. You are comfortable in sharing organizational leadership and decision making with subordinates and prefer to work in a participative atmosphere.	1	2	3	4	5
2. You see a high degree of interdependence as necessary among functions and workers in order to achieve your goals.	1	2	3	4	5
3. The external environment is highly variable and/or changing rapidly and you need the best thinking of all your staff to plan against these conditions.	1	2	3	4	5
4. You feel you need the input of your staff to plan major changes or develop new operating policies and procedures.	1	2	3	4	5

(continued)

		Low		Medium		High
5.	You feel that broad consultation among your people as a group in goals, decisions, and problems is necessary on a continuing basis.	1	2	3	4	5
6.	Members of your management team are (or can become) compatible with each other and are able to create a collaborative rather than a competitive environment.	1	2	3	4	5
7.	Members of your team are located close enough to meet together as needed.	1	2	3	4	5
8.	You feel you need to rely on the ability and willingness of subordinates to resolve critical operating problems directly and in the best interest of the company or organization.	1	2	3	4	5
9.	Formal communication channels are not sufficient for the timely exchange of essential information, views, and decisions among your team members.	1	2	3	4	5
10.	Organization adaptation requires the use of such devices as project management, task forces, and/or ad hoc problem-solving groups to augment conventional organization structure.	1	2	3	4	5
11.	You feel it is important to surface and deal with critical, albeit sensitive, issues that exist in your team.	1	2	3	4	5

		Low		*Medium*		*High*
12.	You are prepared to look at your own role and performance with your team.	1	2	3	4	5
13.	You feel there are operating or interpersonal problems that have remained unsolved too long and need the input from all group members.	1	2	3	4	5
14.	You need an opportunity to meet with your people and set goals and develop commitment to these goals.	1	2	3	4	5

Scoring: If your total score is between 50–70, you are probably ready to go ahead with the team-building program. If your score is between 35–49, you should probably talk the situation over with your team and others to see what would need to be done to get ready for team building. If your score is between 14–34, you are probably not prepared at the present time to start team building.

III. Should you use an outside consultant to help in team building? (Circle appropriate response.)

1.	Does the manager feel comfortable in trying out something new and different with the staff?	Yes	No	?
2.	Is the staff used to spending time in an outside location working on different issues of concern to the work unit?	Yes	No	?
3.	Will group members speak up and give honest data?	Yes	No	?
4.	Does your group generally work together without a lot of conflict or apathy?	Yes	No	?
5.	Are you reasonably sure that the boss is not a major source of difficulty?	Yes	No	?
6.	Is there a high commitment by the boss and unit members to achieve more effective team functioning?	Yes	No	?
7.	Is the personal style of the boss and his or her management philosophy consistent with a team approach?	Yes	No	?

(*continued*)

8. Do you feel you know enough about team building to begin a program without help?   Yes   No   ?
9. Would your staff feel confident enough to begin
   a team-building program without outside help? Yes   No   ?

Scoring: If you have circled six or more "yes" responses, you probably do not
need an outside consultant. If you have four or more "no" responses, you
probably do need a consultant. If you have a mixture of yes, no, and ? responses, you should probably invite in a consultant to talk over the situation
and make a joint decision.

5
BASIC PROGRAMS AND PLANS

Team development is an intervention conducted in a work unit as an action to deal with a condition (or conditions) seen as needing improvement. It is vital to the success of the program that it be the result of a good diagnosis of the needs of the work team; depending on the need, different team-development designs may be appropriate. It would, for example, make little sense to conduct a team-development program designed to improve trust and communications if the problem is a lack of clarity of job assignments or one of general apathy and lack of innovation and energy.

Since diagnosis is dependent on clear and accurate information about the conditions to be improved, the first step is to gather data about the conditions in the system. There may already be certain indications that something is not going well in the work group. Records may show that work output is down, grievances are up, loss time is increasing, quality of work is suffering, or the number of people requesting transfer or quitting is on the increase. Or, the manager may simply become aware that more and more of his or her time is being spent in dealing with people problems.

These initial evidences prompt the manager, executive, or administrator to ponder the questions: Why are these negative trends occurring? What should I begin to do about them?

One underlying assumption regarding teams in organizations is that resources are available in the individuals in the work unit. They have the capability to address and deal with the above questions, and the problems behind these questions, if given the time, encouragement, and freedom needed to work honestly toward solutions. Team development in its best sense is creating the opportunity for people to come together to share their concerns, their ideas, and their experiences, and to begin to work together to solve their mutual problems and achieve common goals.

TEAM DEVELOPMENT AS A DATA-GATHERING, DIAGNOSTIC, ACTION-PLANNING PROCESS

An important perspective in planning the team-development program is to envision the activity as the beginning of a process of getting work-unit members together and involving them in a total program of problem solving and development. Data-gathering, diagnosis, and action-planning activities are the initial steps in a team-development program, with action taking and evaluation as follow-up activities. In this context, the preparations for the team-development program are very simple. The manager communicates either verbally or in written form the following: "I find certain indications that we are not achieving the kinds of personal or collective results that we would like. [Here the manager may be wise to identify such indicators.] I think we should come together and spend some time examining our own activities and begin to plan for our own improvement. I would like to start with a two-day development program. Let us all come prepared to deal with the following questions: (1) What keeps us from being as effective a unit as we could be? (2) What problems do you experience that we should work on? (3) What changes do you feel we need to make to be more effective?"

With this introduction, the group members begin to make the necessary psychological and informational preparations. Generally, a team development process is going to be more effective if the following conditions are present.

Cognitive Understanding.   People are usually more willing to commit themselves to expending their time and energy on an activity if they clearly understand what they are doing and why they are doing it. Prior to beginning the team-development program, it would be well to spend time with the staff discussing the rationale behind team development, clarifying the activities that will be involved, agreeing on the time demands, and arriving at a commitment of all group members to participate. Since it is difficult to build a team if certain members are absent, every person who is an integral member of the team should be involved. This means they should be committed psychologically to participate and the program scheduled at times when all can be present.

Membership Attendance.   Ordinarily a team-development program involves a complete working unit—those people who report to a common superior; whose work connects them with each other; and who must have at least a minimal degree of coordination, common planning, shared goals, and shared decision making in order for them to get work done. Should secretaries or office assistants be included? This depends on the role of that person in the work of the unit. Some secretaries are pure functionaries; they do only work that is assigned. Others are an extension of their bosses and are involved in setting schedules, making decisions, and carrying out action. If everyone recognizes the person as a member whose absence would affect the results of the team effort, that person should be included.

Usually the team represents only one level of an organization—a manager and his or her subordinates. However, organizations vary greatly in their organization structures and operations and, in some systems, mixed levels more accurately represent the working team composition.

The number of people is also a factor to consider. A group of 25–30 might be difficult to manage in a design that calls for each person to clarify his or her job and expectations. However, in a design centered around identifying problems and working out solutions in subgroups, that many people could be handled without major difficulty.

A general rule of thumb about who to include and how many to have would be: When in doubt—include them. It's far better to have a few more in the program than to leave someone out who feels he or she should belong or be included in the department plans.

LENGTH AND LOCATION OF PROGRAM

Team development should be thought of as an ongoing process, not as a single event. People who want to get away for a couple of days and "do team building" with the idea that they will then return to doing business as usual have an incorrect notion of the purpose of team building. The whole program is designed to alter the way an integrated unit functions together. This change is *started* at an initial meeting and continues through the next several months or years until the group really learns to function as a team.

The team-development process often starts with a block of time devoted to helping the group look at its current level of team functioning and devising more effective ways of working together. This initial data-sharing, diagnosis and action-planning sequence takes time and should not be crammed into a couple of hours. Ideally, the members of the work group could plan to meet for at least one full day, and preferably two days, for the initial program. A common format is to meet for dinner, have an evening session, and then meet all the next day or for however long a time has been set aside.

Most team-building facilitators would prefer to have a longer block of time (up to three days) to begin a team-development program. This may not be practical in some situations and modifications must be made. Since we are thinking of team development as an ongoing process, it is possible to start with shorter amounts of time regularly scheduled over a period of several weeks. Some units have successfully conducted a program that opened with an evening meeting, followed by a two- to four-hour meeting each week for the next several weeks. Commitment to the process, regular attendance, high involvement, and good use of time are all more important than length of time.

It is customary to hold the initial team-development program away from the work site. The argument given is that if people meet at the work location, they will find it difficult to "turn off" their day-to-day concerns in order to concentrate fully on the goals of the program. This argument is compelling, even though there is little research evidence regarding the effect of the location on learning and change. Most practitioners do prefer to have development programs at a location where they can have people's full time and attention.

USE OF A CONSULTANT

A common question managers ask is, "Should I conduct the team development effort on my own or should I get an outside person to help us?" "Outside person" could mean either a consultant from outside the organization or an internal consultant who is employed by the organization but is outside the work unit planning the team-development program. A checklist for assessing the need for a consultant is found on p. 36. Ultimately, the manager should be responsible for the development of the work team. The consultant's job is to get that process started.

The use of a consultant is generally advisable if a manager is aware of problems, feels he or she may be one of the problems facing the work unit, is not sure exactly what to do or how to do it, but feels strongly that some positive action is necessary to pull the work group together for more effective operation.

THE ROLES OF THE MANAGER AND THE CONSULTANT

Ultimately, the development of a work team that can regularly stop and critique itself and plan for its improvement lies in the domain of management. It is the manager's responsibility to keep a finger on the pulse of his or her own organization and plan appropriate actions if the work unit shows signs of stress, ineffectiveness, or operating difficulty.

Unfortunately, many managers have not yet been trained to do the data gathering, diagnosis, planning, and action taking required to continually maintain and improve their teams. The role of the consultant is to work with the manager to the point that the manager is capable of engaging in team-development activities as a regular part of his managerial responsibilities. The manager and the consultant (either an external or internal consultant) should form their own two-person team in working through the initial team-building program, always with the following in mind: (1) the manager will be responsible for all team-building activities, although he or she may use the consultant's resources; and (2) the end result of the work of the consultant is to leave the manager capable of continuing the team-development processes without the assistance of the consultant or with minimum consultation help.

THE TEAM-BUILDING CYCLE

Ordinarily a team-building program will follow a cycle similar to that depicted in the accompanying diagram. The whole program begins because someone recognizes a problem or problems. Either before or during the team-building effort, data are gathered to determine the causes of the problem. The data are then analyzed and a diagnosis is made of what is wrong and what is causing the problem. Following the diagnosis, the work unit engages in appropriate planning and problem solving. Actions are planned and assignments made. The plans are then put into action and the results honestly evaluated.

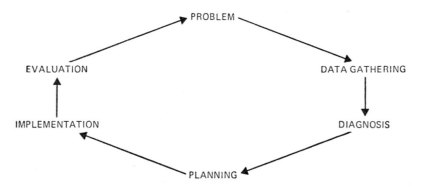

The manager and the consultant will work together in carrying through the program from the time the problem has been identified through some form of evaluation.

Data Gathering

Since team development is essentially a program for training a staff to do its own problem solving, and since a critical condition for effective problem solving is accurate data, a major concern of the manager-consultant team is to gather clear data as to the "causes" behind the symptoms or problems originally identified. The consultant may initially assist in the data gathering, but eventually a team should develop the skill, so it can collect its own data as a basis for working on its own problems. Following are some common data-gathering devices.

Interviews.   At times, the consultant can perform a useful service by interviewing the members of the staff or unit. The consultant is trying to determine the factors behind the problem(s) in order to pinpoint those conditions that may need to be changed or improved. In these interviews, the consultant will often explore the following areas: (a) Why is this unit having the kinds of problems it has? (b) What keeps you personally from being as effective as you would like to be? (c) What things do you like best about this department or unit—things you want to continue? (d) What changes would make you and this unit more effective? (e) How could this unit begin to work more effectively together as a productive team?

Following the interviews, a common practice is to have the consultant do a content analysis of the interviews, identify the major "themes" or suggestions that emerge, and prepare a summary presentation. At the team-building meeting the consultant would then present this summary and the unit, under the manager's direction, would engage in analyzing the data and in action planning to deal with the major concerns.

Some consultants prefer *not* to conduct interviews prior to the team-building meeting and do not want to present a data summary. They have found that information shared in a private interview with a consultant is not as readily discussed in the open with all other team members present, especially if some of those members have been the object of some of the interview information. Consultants have painfully discovered that people will often deny their own interviews, fight the data, and refuse to use it as a basis of discussion and planning. An alternative form of data gathering to interviewing is open data sharing.

Open Data Sharing.   This method asks each person in the unit to share data publicly with the other group members. The data shared may not be as inclusive as that revealed in an interview, but each person feels responsible to "own up" to the information he or she presents to the group and to deal with the issues raised. To prevent forced disclosure, one good ground rule is to tell people that they should raise only those issues they feel they can honestly discuss with the others. People will generally present only the information they feel comfortable discussing; thus, the open sharing of data may result in less information, but more willingness to "work the data."

The kinds of questions suggested above for the interview format are the same ones that people share openly at the beginning of the team-building session. Each presents his or her views on what keeps the unit from being as effective as it could be or suggests reasons for a particular problem. Each person also describes the things he or she likes about the unit, those things that hinder personal effectiveness, and the changes he or she feels would be helpful. All of the data are compiled on a flip chart or chalk board. Following this, the group moves on to the next stage of the team-building cycle.

Diagnosis and Evaluation of Data

With all of the data now available, the manager and consultant must work with the group to summarize the data—i.e., put the information into a priority listing. The summary categories should be listed as either: A—those issues we can work on in this meeting; B—those issues that someone else must work (and identify who the others would be); or C—those issues that apparently are not open to change—things we must learn to accept or live with.

Category A items become the top agenda items for the rest of the team-building session. Category B items are those where strategies must be developed for involving others. And, for category C items, the group must plan coping mechanisms. If the manager is prepared, he or she can handle the summary and the category development process. If the manager feels uneasy about this, the consultant may function as a role model to show how this is done.

The next important step is to review all of the data and to try to identify underlying factors that may be related to several problems. A careful analysis of the data may show that certain procedures, rules, or job assignments are causing several disruptive conditions.

Problem Solving and Planning

After the agenda has been developed out of the data, the roles of the manager and consultant diverge. The manager should move directly into the customary managerial role of group leader. The issues identified should become problems to solve and plans for action should be developed.

While the manager is conducting the meeting, the consultant functions as a group observer and facilitator. Schein has referred to this activity as "process consulting,"[1] a function that others in the group can also learn to handle. In this role, the consultant helps the group look at its problem solving and work processes. He or she may stop the group if certain task or maintenance group functions are missing or being poorly performed. If the group gets bogged down or "steamrollered" into uncommitted decisions, the consultant helps look at these processes, why they occur, and how they can be avoided in the future. In this role, the consultant is training the group to develop more group problem-solving and collaborative action-taking skills.

Implementation and Evaluation

If the actions planned at the team-building session are to make any difference, they must be put into practice. This has always been a major function of management—to see that plans are implemented. The manager must be committed to the team plans; without this commitment, it is unlikely that a manager can be effective in holding people responsible for assignments agreed on in the team-building meeting.

The consultant's role is to observe the degree of action during the implementation phase and to be particularly active during the evaluation period. Another data-gathering process now begins, for that is the basis of evaluation. It is important to see if the actions planned or the goals developed during the team-building time have been achieved. This again should ultimately be the responsibility of the manager, but the consultant can be a help in training the manager to carry out good program evaluation.

CONCLUSION

The manager and the consultant should work closely together in any team-development effort. It is an ineffective program if the manager turns the whole effort over to the consultant with the plea, "You're the expert. Why don't you do it for me?" Such action leads to a great deal of dependency on the consultant, and, if the consultant is highly

---

1   Edgar H. Schein, *Process Consultation* (Reading, Mass.: Addison-Wesley, 1969).

effective, it can cause the manager to feel inadequate or even more dependent. If the consultant is ineffective, the manager can then reject the plans developed as being unworkable or useless, and the failure of the team-building program is blamed on the consultant.

Managers should manage the enterprise. Consultants work with managers to help them do the planning and the action taking in unfamiliar areas where the manager may need some assistance in developing the skill and risk-taking attitude required to move into a new, potentially more profitable activity.

The consultant must be honest, aggressively forthright, and sensitive. He or she must be able to help the manager look at his or her own style and impact in either facilitating or hindering team effectiveness. The consultant needs to help group members get important data out in the open and keep them from feeling overly threatened for sharing with others. The consultant's role involves helping the group develop skills in group problem solving and planning, and, to do this, he or she must have a good feel for group processes and be willing to have the group look at its own dynamics. Finally, the consultant must feel a sense of pride and accomplishment when the manager and the team demonstrate their ability to problem solve independently and thus no longer need a consultant's services.

6
DESIGN OPTIONS: AN OVERVIEW

GOALS AND DESIGN OPTIONS IN TEAM DEVELOPMENT

The overall goal of any team-development program is to improve the effectiveness of a group that must work together to achieve results. Argyris[1] has identified three conditions he feels are characteristic of an effective organization or organizational unit: (1) the ability to gather relevant data; (2) the ability to make sound, free, and informed choices or decisions; and (3) the ability to implement those decisions with commitment. Given these guidelines, the team-building effort would concentrate on building such skills into the organization.

Another way of describing a team-building program is that its purpose is to help the work unit engage in a constant process of self-examination (data gathering) to continually be aware of those conditions that keep the unit from functioning effectively. Having gathered the data, the work group learns how to use the data for making decisions, and then takes those actions that will lead to a growing state of health. Team development, in this sense, is a continual, ongoing process—not just a one-time activity.

As discussed earlier, team development often begins with a block of time (usually two or three days) during which the team starts learn-

---

1 C. Argyris, *Intervention Theory and Method* (Reading, Mass.: Addison-Wesley, 1970).

ing how to engage in its own review, analysis, action planning, decision making, and even action taking.

Following the first meeting, the team may periodically take other blocks of time to continue the process—to see what progress has been made since the last team meeting and to determine what additional changes, training, and planning should be done to improve overall effectiveness. It is also possible that, in time, the team will develop its skills for development to such a point that team members are continually aware of areas that need improvement and raise them at appropriate times with the appropriate people, thereby making it unnecessary to set aside a special time for such action.

There is no one way to put together a team-building program. The format will depend on the experience, interests, and needs of the team members, the experience and needs of the manager, the skills of the consultant, and the nature of the situation that has prompted the meeting.

Following are a range of design alternatives for each phase of a team-building program. Those planning such an activity may wish to select various design elements from among the alternatives which seem applicable to their own situation.

PREPREPARATION PHASE

This phase has been described in the previous chapter on planning the program and need not be reviewed in detail here. In general, the program must be well conceived and those involved must have indicated at least a minimal commitment to participate. Commitment will be increased if people understand clearly *why* the team-building program is being proposed and if they have an opportunity to influence the decision to go ahead with the program.

If this is the first time this group has ever spent some time together with the specific assignment to review their group effectiveness and to plan for change, there is likely to be a good deal of anxiety and apprehension. People will probably have in their minds such questions as:

- Is this really going to do any good?

- Am I going to be "hurt" as a result of what happens?

- Should I get involved or play it close to the vest?

- What is the "real" reason we're spending all this time?

- Will the other people open up and share all the things I know they have complained about in private?

- What will happen if we open up issues nobody can handle?

- Will this jeopardize my relationship with the boss and my co-workers, and create more problems than results?

Questions of such deep concern probably will not be eliminated, but may be reduced as a climate is set and as people "test the water" and find that plunging in is not all that awesome. Experience will be the best teacher and people will allay or confirm their fears as the sessions proceed. Those conducting the session may anticipate such concerns and can raise them prior to the first meeting to reduce any extreme anxiety by openly describing what will happen and what the hoped-for outcome will be.

Alternative Actions

1. Have an outside person interview each unit member to identify problems, concerns, and needs for change.

2. Invite in a speaker to talk about the role of teams in organization and the purposes of team development.

3. Gather data on the level of team effectiveness. (See the instrument at the end of this chapter.)

4. Have a general discussion at a staff meeting about the need for a team-building program.

5. Invite in a manager who has had a successful team-building experience to describe the activities and results in his or her unit.

Goals: The goals of this phase are to explain the purposes of team building, get commitment for participation, and do preliminary work for the workshop.

START-UP PHASE

During this part of a team-development workshop, people come together and begin the process of establishing a climate for work. The climate established will, of course, influence the rest of the program.

Alternative I

1. The superior can give a short opening talk, reviewing the goals as he or she sees them and the need for the program, emphasizing his or her support, and reaffirming the norm that no negative sanctions are intended for any open, honest behavior.

2. The role of the consultant, if there is one, can be explained either by the manager or the consultant.

3. Participants may fill out and share their immediate here-and-now feelings about the meetings by responding to the following questions handed out on a sheet of paper. They call out their answers (to set the norm of open sharing of data) and the person at the flip chart records:

1. How confident are you that any real change will result from these meetings?

1	2	3	4	5
Not confident at all		Some confidence		High confidence

2. To what degree do you feel the people really want to be here and work on team-development issues?

1	2	3	4	5
Don't really want to be here		Some interest in being here		High interest in being here

3. How willing do you think people are to actually make changes that may be suggested?

1	2	3	4	5
Will be un-willing to change		Some willingness to change		Very willing to change

4. How willing do you think you and others will be to express real feelings and concerns?

1	2	3	4	5
Not very willing		Some degree of willingness		Very willing

For a group of eight people, the tabulated data, gathered and presented before the group, might look like this. The profile line is a connection of quickly estimated means.

1.	1_I	2_{II}	x 3_{IIII}	4	5	
2.	1	2	3_{III} x	4_{III}	5_I	
3.	1	2_{II}	x 3_{IIII}	4_I	5	
4.	1_I	2_{II}	x 3_{IIII}	4_I	5	

The group of eight could then be subdivided into two groups of four and asked to discuss: Why is this profile rather low, and what would have to be done here to increase the positive orientation of people towards these meetings?

Subgroups then discuss for twenty minutes and report back to the total group. The purpose of this type of beginning is to set the norm that the whole program is centered on data gathering, data analysis, open sharing, and trying to plan with data. This also allows group members to test the water about here-and-now data rather than more sensitive work-group issues, to see how people will respond and react to the questions.

Alternative II

After preliminary remarks by the manager, the group members could be asked: In order for us to get a picture of how you see our group functioning, would each of you take a few minutes to describe our group as a kind of animal or combination of animals, a kind of machine, a kind of person, or whatever image comes to mind.

Some groups in the past have been described as:

a) A hunting dog—a pointer: we run around and locate problems, then stop and point and hope somebody else will take the action.

b) A Cadillac with pedals: we look good on the outside, but there is no real power to get us moving.

c) A Rube Goldberg device: everything looks crazy and you can't imagine anything will ever happen, but, in some way, for some reason, we do get results at the end.

d) An octopus: each tentacle is out grasping anything it can, but doesn't know what the other tentacles are doing.

As people share these images and explain what elicits the image, the questions are asked: What are the common elements in these images? Do we like these images of ourselves? What do we need to do to change our image? The answering of these questions becomes the major agenda item for subsequent group meetings.

A variation of the above is to have subgroups of two to four people build a collage. They are given magazines and other materials, crayons, magic markers, and a large piece of cardboard and then asked to assemble a collage representing their work unit. The collages are then displayed and explained, and questions similar to those above are asked and then used as a basis for subsequent work.

Alternative III

In this design, the group is asked, usually by the consultant, to work on a major decision-making problem (NASA exercise, Subarctic or Desert Survival, etc.)[2] and to function under the direction of the superior in a fashion similar to the way they work on problems back home. The consultant acts as a process observer. After the exercise, the consultant gets the group members to review their own processes and determine their strengths in problem solving, as well as their deficiencies. The consultant shares with the group his or her observations. Lists of positive and negative features are compiled. The agenda for the following sessions is set: How do we maximize our strengths and overcome our deficiencies? For example, if the process review indicates that the group is very dependent on the leader, that some people are overwhelmed by the "big talker," and that the group jumps to decisions before everyone has a chance to put in ideas, the agenda is how to reduce or change these negative conditions.

Goals: The goals of this phase are to create a climate for work; to get people relaxed and loosened up; to establish norms for being open, for planning, and for dealing with issues; and to present a cognitive framework for the whole experience.

---

2   See the exercises from *Experimental Learning Methods,* 39818 Plymouth Road, Plymouth Michigan 48170.

GROUP PROBLEM-SOLVING
AND PROCESS-ANALYSIS PHASE

Whatever the start-up method, or combination of methods used, the next phase usually involves two parts: (1) the work unit begins to engage in the problem-solving process; and (2) a process consultant or observer helps the group to look at its skill in working on problems as an effective team, as a prelude to improving its problem-solving capabilities.

The McGregor and Likert characteristics (see Chapter 2) of an effective group become useful checklists for the group observer. The process consultant is usually trying to see to what extent the group is effective at both task activities and relationship-maintaining activities. Ineffective teams will often be characterized by such conditions as:

- domination by the leader
- warring cliques or subgroups
- unequal participation and uneven use of group resources
- rigid or dysfunctional group norms and procedures
- a climate of defensivenss or fear
- uncreative alternatives to problems
- restricted communications
- avoidance of differences or potential conflicts.

Such conditions would reduce the team's ability to work together in collective problem-solving situations. The role of the consultant would be to help the group become aware of its processes and begin to develop greater group skills. Specifically, after becoming aware of a process problem, the group needs to establish a procedure, guideline, or plan of action to reduce the negative condition.

Alternative I

Following the opening remarks, the consultant, outside person, or manager presents data that have been collected from the group members via interviews or instruments prior to the meeting. The group is asked to analyze the data: What do the data mean? Why do we respond the way we do? What conditions give rise to negative responses? What do we need to change to get a more positive response to our own organization?

This analysis can best be done in subgroups (three to four people) and then shared and compiled into a total listing of issues and possible change actions. The summaries form the basis for the subsequent sessions. The group also puts the data into categories as described earlier. The category A items are the major work issues on the agenda.

Alternative II

This design requires some extensive case analysis prior to the team-building sessions. An external consultant, a company OD person, or someone in management pulls together from one to several case studies, vignettes, or critical incidents that seem to represent some reoccurring problems in the work unit. Another possibility is to have each member write up a short case that represents a problem area for him or her. Again, the group task is to look at the several cases, try to discover what the underlying conditions are that trigger off such conditions, and then plan action for reducing the likelihood that such conditions would occur again.

Alternative III

In this method, objective data gathered from records in the work unit are compiled and presented to the group members. Such information as the production records, grievance rate, absenteeism, turnover, lost time, budget discrepancies, late reports, cost increases, and so on are included in this feedback. The group's job is to conduct an in-depth analysis of the data, diagnose the course of negative trends, and then engage in action planning for improvement.

Alternative IV

Instead of data from prior data-collection methods being presented to the group, data about the conditions or problems of the team are surfaced at the team meeting. Each person is asked to come prepared to share his or her perception of the following: (1) What keeps this work group from functioning at its maximum potential? (2) What keeps you, personally, from doing the kind of job you would like to do? (3)

What things do you like in this unit that you want to have maintained? (4) What changes would you like to see made that would help you and the whole group?

Group members each take a turn sharing their information. The responses are listed on newsprint and common themes are identified. The most important issues are listed in priority and they become the items for discussion.

Problem-Solving Process

Regardless of the alternative selected above, the work unit should by this point have identified a series of problems, concerns, or issues. The team next must move into a problem-solving process by engaging in the following actions:

1. Put problems in order of priority and select the five or six most pressing problems to be addressed during the workshop.

2. Begin the classic problem-solving process: problem—alternative solutions—select alternative to be implemented—work out action plan—action—evaluation of results.

3. Work out forcefield analysis.[3] Identify existing level, formulate goal, identify driving and restraining forces, develop plan to remove restraining forces.

4. Begin role negotiations. Negotiate between people or subunits the actions needed from each other to improve effectiveness.

5. Set up task-force teams or subunits. Give each team a problem to work on—set up the actions, carry out the action, and assess the results.

6. After all problems have been listed, the group sorts them out into: (a) Those problems we can work on here; (b) those problems someone else must handle (and identify who that is); (c) those problems we must live with, since they appear to be beyond our ability to change.

---

3   Kurt Lewin, "Group Decision and Social Change," *Readings in Social Psychology*, ed. by Maccoby et al. (New York: Holt, 1958). See also W.G. Dyer, *Insight to Impact, Strategies for Interpersonal and Organizational Change* (Provo, Utah: BYU Press, 1976).

7. Set targets, objectives, or goals. The group spends time identifying short- or long-range goals it wishes to achieve, makes assignments, and sets target dates for completion.

Goals: To begin to take action on the problems identified. To make assignments and set dates for the completion of work. To practice better problem solving, decision making, planning, objective selecting, and delegation skills.

INTERPERSONAL, SUBUNIT, AND GROUP FEEDBACK PHASE

Often, a major issue following the identification of problems is the sharing of feedback to individuals, subparts of the team, or to the work group as a whole. Certain actions, functions, or personal styles and strategies on the part of one or more people may be clogging up the teamwork and preventing goal achievement and satisfaction for certain other team members. If such is the case, it may be legitimate to engage in an open feedback session. The goal is to share data about performance so difficulties can be resolved. It is critical that a feedback session *not* slip into name calling, personal griping, or verbal punishing of others. All feedback given should reflect a genuine willingness to work cooperatively: "My performance suffers because of some things that happen in which you are involved. Let met share my feelings and reactions so you can see what is happening to me. I would like to work out a way that we all can work more productively together."

Feedback is most helpful if it can be given in descriptive fashion, or in the form of suggestions.

Descriptive Feedback.   (Describe behavior or actions, and the impact it has.) Example: "John, when you promise me that you will have a report ready at a certain time (as happened last Thursday) and I don't get it, that really frustrates me. It puts me behind schedule and makes me feel very resentful towards you. Are you aware that such things are going on, and how should we work out this kind of problem?"

Suggestions. "John, let me make a suggestion that would really be of help to me as we work together. If you could get your reports to me on time, particularly those that have been promised at a certain time, it would help my work schedule and reduce my frustration. Also, if I don't get a report on time, what would you prefer I do about it?"

Other Possibilities.   Following are some other ways group members go about sharing feedback with one another.

1. Each person has a sheet of newsprint on the wall. Everyone writes on the sheets of others items in three areas: (a) things we want you to *begin* doing (that will increase your effectiveness); (b) things we want you to *stop* doing; and (c) things we want you to *continue* to do.

2. Envelope exchange. Each person writes a note to others covering the same issues as in item one above and gives the notes to the others.

3. Confirmation-disconfirmation process. Group members summarize how they view themselves and their own work performance—their strengths and areas that need improvement. Others are asked to confirm or disconfirm the person's self diagnosis.

4. Management profile. Each person presents the profile of his or her effectiveness from previously gathered data (from instruments like the BSR Management Profile, Telometrics Profile, Scientific Methods Grid Profile, etc.). Group confirms or disconfirms the profile.

5. Analysis of subunits. Each organization's subunit is discussed in terms of what the unit does well, what it needs to change, and what it needs to improve.

6. Total unit or organizational analysis.[4] The group looks at how it has been functioning and critiques its own performance over the past year. It identifies things it has done well and areas that need improvement.

7. Open feedback session. Each person who would like feedback may ask for it in order to identify areas of personal effectiveness and areas that need improvement.

---

4   Richard Beckhard, "The Confrontation Meeting," *Harvard Business Review* 45 (March-April 1967): 149–155.

8. Prescription writing. Each person writes a prescription for others: "Here is what I would prescribe that you do (or stop doing) in order to be more effective in your position." Prescriptions are then exchanged.

Goals: This phase is designed to share feedback to people in such a way as to help them improve their effectiveness and to give feedback to work units with the same objective in mind.

ACTION-PLANNING PHASE

The end result of all the activities mentioned above is to help the work unit identify those conditions that are blocking both individual and group effectiveness, so that the group may begin to develop plans for action and change. Decisions for action should be made with a commitment to carry such action to completion. During this phase, plans are developed, assignments are given, procedures are outlined, and dates are set for completion and review. Often the plan is a set of agreements regarding who is willing to take a specific action. All such agreements should be written down, circulated, and followed up later to insure they have been carried out.

Below is a set of actions that are possible during the action-planning phase:

1.   Each person takes time to evaluate his or her feedback and develops a plan of action for personal improvement. This plan is presented to the others.

2.   Contract negotiations.[5] If there are particular problems between individuals or subunits, specific agreements for dealing with conflict issues are drawn up and signed.

3.   Assignment summary. Each person summarizes what his or her assignments are and the actions he or she intends to take as a follow-up of the team-development meeting.

---

5   Roger Harrison, "Role Negotiations: A Tough-Minded Approach to Team Development," in W. Burke and H. Hornstein, *The Social Technology of Organization Development* (Washington, D.C., NTL Learning Resources, 1971).

4. Subunit or group plans. If development plans have been completed, such plans are presented and reviewed.

5. Schedule review. The group looks at its time schedule and its action plans. Dates for completion and dates for giving progress reports on work being done are confirmed. Schedule for the next staff meeting is set. If another team-development workshop or meeting is needed, it may be scheduled at this time.

Goals: The goal of this phase is to confirm and pinpoint changes, goals, assignments, and dates for completion.

FOLLOW-UP PHASE

Unless the decisions made and actions planned are actually implemented, the functioning of the team will not improve. It is important that follow-up meetings are scheduled and a review conducted of decisions and actions. The manager in charge must manage the follow-up efforts. If a good three-day team-building meeting is held, but the excitement and enthusiasm that is generated is allowed to dissipate because of a lack of follow through, there is the danger that the level of effectiveness of the work unit will decrease and the team-building meetings will have had, in the long run, a negative effect.

In the follow-up phase, certain alternative courses of action are possible:

1. Process review. At the end of the workshop, time may be taken to critique the team-development program—things that went well, things that need to be changed, recommendations for the next team-development meeting, and so on.

2. Management review and follow-through. All assignments and action plans are reviewed by appropriate managers or management groups to make sure these plans are supported and reviewed, and that commitments called for at appropriate dates have been set.

3. Task forces or committees may have been formed. Specific dates are set to have these work groups report on the results of their efforts.

4. Following the initial team-building meeting, shorter periods of time may be used to have a continuation of the first team-building meeting. It may be possible to have a four-hour block to review the work done since the last meeting, gather new data, make new assignments and plan for the next session. Team building in this manner becomes an ongoing process.

Goals: The major goals in this phase are to establish a system that will insure that actions agreed on and agreements made are, in fact, implemented. Clear deadlines are set and the regular processes of management are followed to insure completion. A major goal is to see that continual team building becomes a part of the ongoing activities of the work group.

Keeping in mind the many design options and alternatives we have discussed, consider the following case example of an organization that engaged in a team-development program.

ILLUSTRATIVE CASE: WMBA AND CHANNEL 12

When the staff of a broadcast system composed of radio station WMBA and TV channel 12 began a major organization improvement effort, it was the result of several months of thinking and planning. Bruce Chamberlain, the station manager, had been extremely conscious of a loss of revenues, harder times in selling TV and radio spots, and evidence of a drop-off in listening and viewing publics. There were indications that the radio and TV groups were at odds with each other, program materials were not as creative as they used to be, and the sales staff seemed to be dragging its collective feet.

Bruce reviewed these conditions with the managers who reported to him. The total station staff fluctuated between forty and sixty people, depending on the season and work load, and was divided into the major groupings of radio, TV, production, sales, personnel, finances, and smaller special groups in FM radio, special effects and projects, and public service. A managers' meeting was held each week and Chamberlain had suggested that the whole station needed to review its overall activities to see how all phases of their operations could improve. Bruce had contacted a nearby university and found a professor knowledgeable in organization development methods who had met with him and outlined a series of alternatives. Since the station management group annually got together for a kind of retreat for business and social reasons, Bruce felt that this time could be better used to seriously review their entire organization, do some more effective planning and coordination, and iron out some of the interface problems.

This proposal was discussed at length in the managers' meeting and finally agreed to. The dates were set, location agreed on, a decision was made to hire an outside resource person, and a committee was set up to make all detailed arrangements.

The outside person met with the managers at a later meeting and outlined the purpose of such a two-day program. The managers suggested issues they would like addressed, the consultant reviewed several possible design arrangements, and it was agreed that the committee assigned (which included Chamberlain) would work with the consultant in making final program plans. Notice of the meeting was shared with all station personnel, and those who were to participate received both a verbal and written invitation. They were asked to come prepared to review the total functioning of the broadcast system and to spend time giving their suggestions for improving the entire system.

The initial session began on Wednesday evening and the program was to end at 3:00 P.M. on Friday. Following dinner, the Wednesday evening session began at 7:30. Chamberlain first outlined the need for the session as he saw it and noted some problems he hoped to address. The consultant was introduced and her role clarified—she would handle some parts of the program, present some lecture inputs, direct some activities, and be a process observer. The group was then asked to break into four subgroups, with four or five people in each group. Eighteen people had been invited to this session. This group included the key management, supervisory, and administration people who all worked quite closely together.

The subgroups were asked to think about the overall broadcasting system and to come up with an animal, vehicle, general image, or any combination of things that would best describe the organization as they saw it.

In the groups there was a lot of laughter as people came up with wild ideas. After a half hour, each group shared its images with the rest. The images that everyone agreed were most appropriate were:

a) The organization was like a combination dog—a pointer-setter-terrier. It would point at flaws or problems; it would sit down and wait for someone to do something; and it would yelp like a terrier if anyone did anything out of the ordinary.

b) The organization was like a kaleidoscope. Lots of beautiful images were created, but with just a slight turn of anything the image would change. Nothing was very stable or constant, but the picture always looked good to an outside observer.

Individuals were asked to do some private planning that evening and work in the small groups again in the morning. The topics: What do we do that makes us feel we have the image we think we have? What are our biggest problems as an organization? What do we need to do to alter our image and deal with our problem areas?

The next morning the small groups met for nearly two hours. When the groups came together and combined their data, the list of issues was sobering. The major concerns were: (1) too much time was spent trying to please the board of directors and not enough attention was being paid to the public; (2) each area was fighting with others, trying to "build a kingdom" rather than sharing ideas and information; (3) staff meetings were bull sessions rather than productive working periods; (4) people were trying to pad budgets and expenses; (5) those who had to serve TV, radio, and FM in special staff capacities were not clear as to priorities, time commitments, or assignments; (6) there was a tendency to put blame for problems on someone else—nobody ever admitted any problems in one's own area; (7) a major goal was to try to look good on paper—have everything in order without being concerned about quality performance.

The total group arranged the seven major problem areas into a priority list of work items. The group was now reformed into four new work groups and each group was given a problem to manage. These new groups were carefully formed to make sure that a cross-section of people from all departments was included in each unit. Each group was asked to take the problem assigned and come up with the following: (1) What specific actions should be taken to deal with the problem area? (2) Who should be responsible for the actions (give specific names)? (3) Who should be responsible for supervising or managing the actions? (4) When should the actions start and end? (5) What would be the date for the first report of results? (6) What rewards or penalties should be expected for success or failure to take action?

The groups worked hard at their tasks and late in the day they all came together to get the first group report. There was a serious discussion about the proposals made. People had to agree to assignments, deadlines, and the rewards and penalties. The consultant (who had been a roving observer and facilitator to the small groups) actively helped the group to look at the way it arrived at its final decisions. In addition, some problems in factions blocking each other, reactions to Chamberlain, and low commitment had to be worked out. But the group plugged away at the task until a final set of actions, to which all agreed, had been developed for every problem area.

By Friday afternoon the staff was tired, but very satisfied. They had a complete list of action assignments with deadlines and dates for reporting progress. More importantly, they had experienced the satisfaction of honestly facing their real problems for the first time and felt successful in being able to work together in arriving at solutions that made sense to them. Many commented that this was the best work session they had ever had, and there was a sense of confidence that they could handle future problems more easily.

Team Development Scale by William G. Dyer

1. To what extent do I feel a real part of the team?

1	2	3	4	5
Completely a part all the time	A part most of the time	On the edge, sometimes in, sometimes out	Generally outside, except for one or two short periods	On the outside, not really a part of the team

2. How safe is it in this team to be at ease, relaxed, and myself?

1	2	3	4	5
I feel perfectly safe to be myself, they won't hold mistakes against me.	I feel most people would accept me if I were completely myself, but there are some I am not sure about.	Generally, you have to be careful what you say or do in this team.	I am quite fearful about being completely myself in this team.	A person would be a fool to be himself in this team.

3. To what extent do I feel "under wraps," that is, have private thoughts, unspoken reservations, or unexpressed feelings and opinions that I have not felt comfortable bringing out into the open?

1	2	3	4	5
Almost completely under wraps	Under wraps many times	Slightly more free and expressive than under wraps	Quite free and expressive much of the time	Almost completely free and expressive

4. How effective are we, in our team, in getting out and using the ideas, opinions, and information of all team members in making decisions?

1	2	3	4	5

1	2	3	4	5
We don't really encourage everyone to share their ideas, opinions, and information with the team in making decisions.	Only the ideas, opinions, and information of a few members are really known and used in making decisions.	Sometimes we hear the views of most members before making decisions and sometimes we disregard most members.	A few are sometimes hesitant about sharing their opinions, but we generally have good participation in making decisions.	Everyone feels his or her ideas, opinions, and information are given a fair hearing before decisions are made.

5. To what extent are the goals the team is working toward understood and to what extent do they have meaning for you?

1	2	3	4	5
I feel extremely good about goals of our team.	I feel fairly good, but some things are not too clear or meaningful.	A few things we are doing are clear and meaningful.	Much of the activity is not clear or meaningful to me.	I really do not understand or feel involved in the goals of the team.

6. How well does the team work at its tasks?

1	2	3	4	5
Coasts, loafs, makes no progress	Makes a little progress, most members loaf	Progress is slow, spurts of effective work	Above average in progress and pace of work	Works well, achieves definite progress

7. Our planning and the way we operate as a team is largely influenced by:

1	2	3	4	5
One or two team members	A clique	Shifts from one person or clique to another	Shared by most of the members, some left out	Shared by all members of the team

(continued)

8. What is the level of responsibility for work in our team?

1	2	3	4	5
Each person assumes personal responsibility for getting work done.	A majority of the members assume responsibility for getting work done.	About half assume responsibility, about half do not.	Only a few assume responsibility for getting work done.	Nobody (except perhaps one) really assumes responsibility for getting work done.

9. How are differences or conflicts handled in our team?

1	2	3	4	5
Differences or conflicts are denied, suppressed, or avoided at all cost.	Differences or conflicts are recognized, but remain unresolved mostly.	Differences or conflicts are recognized and some attempts are made to work them through by some members, often outside the team meetings.	Differences and conflicts are recognized and some attempts are made to deal with them in our team.	Differences and conflicts are recognized and the team usually is working them through satisfactorily.

10. How do people relate to the team leader, chairman, or "boss"?

1	2	3	4	5
The leader dominates the team and people are often fearful or passive.	The leader tends to control the team, although people generally agree with the leader's direction.	There is some give and take between the leader and the team members.	Team members relate easily to the leader and usually are able to influence leader decisions.	Team members respect the leader, but they work together as a unified team with everyone participating and no one dominant.

11. What suggestions do you have for improving our team functioning?

7
DEVELOPING THE NEW TEAM

Team building is not a method used exclusively to develop an existing unit that wants to improve its effectiveness; it is also a method that can help a completely new unit mold a group of "strangers" into a more workable team. New teams may either be temporary or a more permanent nature. Most organizations, at one time or another, use various types of ad hoc groups, formed for a specific task and often for a limited duration. These are variously called "task forces," "committees," "work groups," "project groups," etc. In addition, when a new department is formed or units merge, a new working group that will function over a long period of time is created. In either case, the problem facing the unit is: How can we establish the kind of foundation, procedures, and programs that will maximize the possibility that we will be able to work together successfully?

The major tasks facing the new team are basically the same as one that has worked together—that is, they must build a relationship, establish a facilitative emotional climate, and work out methods for (1) setting goals, (2) solving problems, (3) making decisions, (4) insuring follow through and completion of tasks, (5) developing collaboration of effort, (6) establishing lines of open communication, and (7) insuring an appropriate support system that will let people feel accepted and yet keep issues open for discussion and disagreement. The advantage the new team has over an old established unit in a team-building situation is that it does not have to break down any barriers, bad habits, nonuseful stereotypes or attitudes, inappropriate working relations, or procedures that have been formed and are sometimes set rigidly in the concrete of human habit. In a new unit where members have had some previous working relationships, there may be some residues of ineffective feelings or actions that may need to be handled. Generally the new team can start its activities by asking: How can we set in motion the kinds of actions that will allow us to work together and get our goals accomplished and leave us feeling good about ourselves and each other?

THE EFFECTIVE COMMITTEE

If we take a newly formed committee as an example of a unit interested in new team development, there is evidence that people enter into this new assignment with certain positive and negative expectations. One survey of nearly 200 university-based people with committee assignments came up with the following data.

Reasons Why People Do Not Like to Serve on Committees

1. Poor leadership. The leader *fails* to keep the discussion on the subject, to monitor and direct to keep things moving in the appropriate direction, and to engage in those activities that are stimulating and motivating to the members.

2. Goals are unclear. Members are not really sure what they are trying to accomplish.

3. Assignments are not taken seriously by committee members. There is an apparent lack of commitment.

4. There is a lack of clear focus on the committee's assignment—e.g., "What are we supposed to be doing today?"

5. Recommendations of the committee are often ignored by top management. Management needs to be more responsive to the committee.

6. Waste of time. Unproductive discussions of problems, with no conclusions or decisions made.

7. Lack of follow-through with assignments on the part of committee members.

8. Often a domination by one person or clique. Some talk and push for their positions, while others wonder why they are there.

9. Lack of preparation by committee members, including the chairman of the meeting. Agenda not prepared, materials and things that really need to be there are not available. Someone has not done his homework.

10. No action taken. The committee spends a lot of time without coming up with specific items resulting in some kind of action.

11. People often have hidden agendas—personal axes to grind. They get into discussions that only one or two think are important.

Things People Like about Committees When They Function Well

1. Clear role definition of the committee—what the committee and its members are supposed to do, what their goals are.

2. Careful time control. Starting on time and ending on time. Enough time allowed to get the work done and no more.

3. Committee members are sensitive to each other's needs and expressions. People listen and respect others' opinions.

4. An informal relaxed atmosphere, rather than a formal exchange.

5. Good preparation on the part of the chairman and committee members. Materials prepared and available.

6. Members all qualified and interested. They want to be a part of the committee. A definite commitment exists.

7. Interruptions are avoided or held to a minimum.

8. Good minutes or records are kept, so that decisions are not lost. There is no need to search out what decisions were made.

9. Periodically, the committee stops and assesses its own performance. Needed improvements are worked out.

10. Committee members feel they are given some kind of reward for their committee efforts. Recognition and appreciation are given, so that they feel they are really making a contribution.

11. The work of the committee is accepted and used, and seems to make a contribution to the organization.

This survey suggests that it would be wise for the newly formed committee to spend enough time initially planning how it will work to avoid those activities that bother people and how it will incorporate those to which people respond.

DESIGN FOR A NEW COMMITTEE

In this team-building session, members meet long enough for people to get acquainted and to set guidelines and procedures for work.

Step 1: Developing a Realistic Priority Level

It often occurs that people who are put together on a new team —frequently by assignment—have widely differing levels of priority or commitment to the work assigned. Some may see it as a highly significant assignment and worthy of a great deal of time and energy. Others may see it as important, but lower on their personal priority list, while still others may see it as low in both importance and priority. One method for coming to grips with the priority issue is the following:

(a) Have each person draw a vertical line that represents his or her total work requirements and the priorities for them. Each person puts a mark at the point that represents where this team assignment ranks as a priority activity. See Fig. 7.1.

(b) Have each person write down the amount of time he or she would be willing to commit to the work of the team over a month's time.

(c) Summarize the priority rankings (see Fig. 7.1) and also the time commitments. See the range of times and priorities and also the averages for the two dimensions.

(d) In the group, let each person who desires explain his or her priority and time rankings and then come to agreement as to a realistic amount of time and energy that can be expected of the team as a whole. Persons with higher priority and team commitments may be allowed to accept heavier assignments. Making this decision openly reduces the resentment some have for doing more work and the guilt of others for letting them.

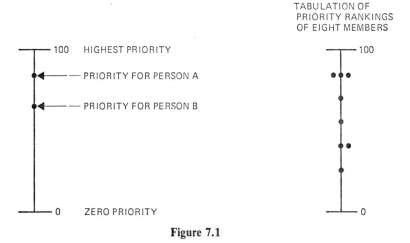

Figure 7.1

Step 2: Sharing Expectations

Give five minutes for each person to think about and get ready to respond to the following questions:

(a) What worries you most or is your biggest concern about working on this team (or committee)?

(b) How would this team function if everything went just as you would hope?

(c) What would this team be like if everything went wrong?

(d) What actions do you think must be taken to insure the positive outcomes?

Each person has an opportunity to share reactions; everyone responds to each question in turn. Try to identify the major concerns people have and list them on a blackboard or newsprint. These concerns should become items on a planning agenda as conditions to take into consideration in order to insure that positive things are achieved.

Step 3: Clarifying Goals

At this point, having now established the priority and commitment level and identified positive and negative expectations, the new team is ready to clarify its goals and objectives.

At one level the team should discuss and then write down what members agree is the *core mission* of the group. This is a statement of the basic function or "reason for being" for that group, committee, or team. All plans and actions should be evaluated against the core mission. The question to constantly ask is: If we continue the activities already outlined, will we accomplish our core mission? Extending from the core mission are the subgoals and specific objectives for a given period of time.

For example, the Edgemont Company formed a task force to review all training and development activities in the company and to come up with some recommendations for a coordinated training and development effort. The task force met and established its core mission: The mission of this task force is to insure an appropriate and effective thrust in management and organization development in the Edgemont Company.

Subgoals were then identified: We will accomplish our core mission by: (a) reviewing all ongoing training and development programs; (b) assessing the effectiveness of these programs; (c) determining if there are any overlaps or major gaps in training and development; (d) constructing a model of an effective program; (e) making recommendations to the executive committee as to the type of program needed; (f) assisting, if needed, in the implementation of the recommendations; and (g) assisting in evaluating the consequences or results of the implemented recommendations.

Having set the core mission and specific subgoals, the task force is now ready to make specific assignments to task-force members.

Step 4: Formulating Operating Guidelines

During this team-building period, the new team needs to establish guidelines for how it will work during the course of its existence. At the same time the guidelines are established, a provision for changing the guidelines if they prove to be dysfunctional or inappropriate as conditions change also needs to be formulated. Following are some of the areas for which guidelines may be useful. The guidelines should clarify actions and roles and should reduce the ambiguity or mixed expectations of people as to how things ought to function, which is the basis of a great deal of conflict in a working group.

1. *How will we make decisions?*   It is useful for the new team to talk about its decision-making procedures. Do they want to make

decisions by a majority vote, a team consensus (to have all decisions made by the total group), or leave some decisions to subgroups that are assigned work?

If the group opts to make decisions by consensus, all should realize that this does not mean unanimity (everyone thinking alike). A consensus decision is a hammered-out decision where everyone is permitted a say. After discussion and give-and-take and compromise has occurred, consensus is reached when people honestly can say, "This is a sound decision—one that I am willing *to support and implement*. It is not exactly what I personally want, but given the range of opinions, the time factor, and the kinds of personalities involved, it is a good, working decision."

Unless *everyone* can take the position described above, a consensus has not been reached. Discussion would need to continue and adjustments or compromises or new alternatives would have to be explored until a solution is found that results in consensus as defined above.

2. *What will be our basic method for work?*   The team should decide what it feels will be the most efficient way to get work done. Should they have all items considered by the total group, have people do individual work that is then submitted to the group, or have sub-committees do the initial work? It is possible that all of the above may be used, depending on the nature of the work to be done. However, the method of work should be decided at the outset.

3. *How do we make sure everyone gets a chance to discuss issues or raise concerns important to him or her?*   If a team is to be effective, members need to feel that they are able to discuss and have considered issues or concerns they deem important. How will the team insure this condition? It may be agreed that any member can put any item of concern on the agenda for the next meeting. There may be an "open" meeting scheduled periodically to allow discussion of any topic or issue. Time could be reserved at the end of certain meetings for an open discussion. Members could be asked to distribute a memo identifying the issue they want discussed.

4. *How will we resolve differences?*   In any working group there will be times when individuals or subgroups disagree. If not handled or managed, disagreements can, at the least, waste time, and may even split the group into warring factions. A guideline for dealing with

differences can be useful. If two people or subgroups disagree, it may be more useful to have a guideline which recommends they get together (sometimes with a mediator) outside of the meeting of the whole group to work out their differences rather than holding up the actions of the total team. A third person or subunit could be appointed to listen to both sides of the issues and then recommend possible compromises or new alternatives. Time limits for the open discussion of differences might expedite reaching a conclusion (or might be a frustrating hindrance). A majority voting procedure might be appropriate if the group can honestly adopt a "loyal opposition" position which allows people the right to disagree or vote differently, but still implement actions.

Whatever the method for discussion, understanding, and resolving issues, a guideline will provide a beginning for coping with the sensitive problem of differences that may occur.

5. *How will we insure the completion of work?*   One of the major problems in working groups (particularly of the committee or task-force variety) is the frustrating experience of some people coming unprepared or failing to complete assignments. How can the team face that issue constructively? The guidelines may suggest that no one will be given or will accept an assignment if the person honestly knows he or she will not invest an appropriate amount of energy in its preparation. This means there must be a realistic level of priority building (see Step 1) and a trusting enough climate that people will feel free to state their honest preferences and reactions to assignments. This guideline may outline a procedure for having the chairman or other designated leader remind every person with an assignment at a suitable time prior to the next meeting. An action summary of every meeting will clearly identify all assignments and dates for report and completion, as illustrated in the sample below:

Action Summary (Sample)

Decision	Who is to do what	Date for completion	Date to report progress
1. It was agreed there would be a training seminar for all supervisors on June 15.	1. John Hicks will make all physical arrangements.	June 10	Next meeting— May 20
	2. Ann Stewart will contact the three possible resource people.	May 24	Next meeting— May 20

The action summary can be used in place of minutes or in addition to regular narrative minutes, but it should clearly pinpoint assignments and times for completion. If a person fails to complete an assignment, the guideline may suggest an appropriate action—e.g., a personal visit by the chairman, a report and explanation to the total committee, or some other review mechanism.

6. *How will we change things that are not producing results?* There should be some guideline for reviewing the way the committee or team has been working and a method for making changes when guidelines or procedures or even people in certain positions are no longer achieving results. This guideline may suggest a periodic evaluation session when the team honestly looks at its own work, reviews its successes and failures, and asks the question, "What changes would make our team more effective?" If guideline 3 has been operating effectively, many issues will have been covered, but the team may need to agree on a periodic review and evaluation meeting, or that any person could call for such a meeting when he or she felt conditions warranted it.

Again, the success of such a meeting depends on people feeling free to express their honest views about the team's effectiveness and to make recommendations for improvement. A fearful, defensive group will find it hard to plan useful changes.

NEW TEAMS IN ACTION

What are the differences between a work group that plans for its own successful functioning and one that plunges into work and hopes everything turns out all right? Consider the following two cases.

The Dean's Council—State University

With the arrival of a new president, a number of positions at the dean's level were changed; new people moved into some positions and reassignments were made for others. When the new academic vice-president met with all of the current deans, his desire was to get the group involved quickly into the matters of concern to the new administration. He spent the first twenty minutes allowing each dean the opportunity to introduce himself or herself and to take two minutes to say something about his or her particular college. As usual, some talked beyond their two minutes, but most kept to the stated limit.

The vice-president then outlined the major tasks of the council as he saw them, asked for everyone's cooperation, and set the time for the next meeting. Much to his dismay, the vice-president discovered that the council did not move ahead as he expected. At nearly every meeting, 30 to 40 percent of the deans were absent and an associate dean was there representing the chief. The functioning of the council was erratic. Sometimes a few people dominated the discussion and the others sat silent; at other times, people seemed divided into two camps and decisions were polarized between these two factions. The vice-president was reluctant to make final decisions that were opposed by such a large number of powerful deans, so he tabled many of the decisions while "further aspects of the problem were investigated." Clearly this group was going to be a tough one to manage.

The Dean's Council—Union University

When the new dean's council was formed, Martha Allen, the recently appointed academic vice-president, spent a lot of time thinking about how to get that group of highly skilled, differentially trained people to work together for common university goals. She asked each dean to clear one full day to meet at a retreat center for planning the way the council would work during the coming year.

At the first meeting in the morning, Allen described what she felt were the major functions of the dean's council and what she hoped they might accomplish. She then asked each dean to stand, introduce himself or herself if new to the group, and share his or her views about the council in regard to two questions: (1) What would the council be like if everything functioned ideally? and (2) What would the council be like if everything went wrong and it was a total disaster? Allen began the process by frankly describing her hopes and fears for the council. Each dean then followed and the comments were very frank and insightful.

Allen then asked the deans to divide into small groups. There were eighteen present, so they divided into three groups of six people. Each group was asked to consider the question: What will we need to do (how shall we organize and how shall we function) in order to ensure that the workings of this council are successful?

After an hour's discussion, the three groups reported back the results of their discussion. Each group listed its recommendations as to the actions needed to ensure success. These included such things as the need for regular meeting times when all can be in attendance, defined agendas announced in advance, subcommittees to deal with continuing problems, regular meetings with the president, an administrative assistant in the vice-president's office to follow up on action items, and clear communications as to changes and developments from the president's office. Almost all of the recommendations were agreed on and action decisions made on those for which a decision was appropriate.

The vice-president then asked the small groups to each take one problem and come up with recommendations. Group 1 was asked to consider: How shall we make decisions in the council? Should all decisions be by majority vote, by consensus, or sometimes one or the other? Group 2 discussed: How shall the council function to ensure open discussion of all issues without getting bogged down in lengthy, unproductive discussions? Group 3 had the assignment: How shall we critique the council's activities to see if we are achieving our goals, and how shall we determine if someone is not satisfied with the way the council is working?

After intensive discussion, the groups presented their recommendations to the total council and a set of operating guidelines were adopted. People left the workshop with a sense of satisfaction about the accomplishments of the day, optimism about the coming year, and a greater feeling of integration with each other and the administration.

New teams do not have to wait until problems arise and the negative consequences force some type of remedial action. A team can plan for its future and build in procedures for continually assessing its own functioning. Given this feedback, it can regularly take actions to ensure the team stays on target with its goals. Such planning is the major goal of a development program for the new team or work unit.

8
ORDER OUT OF CHAOS AND CONFLICT

Sometimes a group has worked together for years, but either basic assignments were never clarified or conditions have changed an old role definitions are no longer adequate. In such situations, another type of team-building effort is needed.

THE ROLE CLARIFICATION MODEL

The role clarification model of team building is considered appropriate if several of the following conditions are prevalent in the organization or unit considering a team-building program.[1]

1. The unit is newly organized and people are not clear as to what others do and what others expect of them.

2. Changes and reassignments have been made in the unit and there is a lack of clarity as to how the various functions and positions now fit together under the new arrangements.

3. Original job descriptions are old. Staff meetings are held infrequently and then only for passing on needed directions. People

---

1   See I. Dayol, and J.M. Thomas, "Operation KPE: Developing A New Organization," *The Journal of Applied Behavioral Science* **4,** no. 4 (1968): 473-506, for a discussion of the RAT Technique, similar to this discussion.

carry out their assignments with very little contact with others in the same office. People generally feel isolated.

4. Conflicts and disruptions between people in the unit seem to be increasing. Coffee-break talk and other information communications center around discussions of overlaps and encroachments on work assignments from others. People get requests they don't understand. People hear about what others are doing via the grapevine and it sounds like something they should know about but nobody gets them together.

5. The boss engages primarily in one-on-one management. Staff meetings are infrequent or are primarily held for hearing the boss raise issues with one individual at a time while others watch and wait for their turn. Almost no problem solving is done as a total staff or between people. Issues are taken to the boss and only then are needed people called together.

6. People sit in their offices and wonder, "What is happening in this outfit? I don't know what others are doing and I'm sure nobody knows (or cares) what I'm doing."

7. A crisis occurs because everyone thought someone else was responsible for handling a situation that was never covered.

PLANNING

Once a group has diagnosed the need for a team building effort, the next step is to develop an action plan.

Time Commitment. Assuming a staff of eight to ten people, the minimum time needed is approximately one hour for each person or a total of eight to ten hours of meeting time—preferably one solid block of time. Assuming a training day from 8:30 to 12:00 and 1:00 to 4:30, this could be achieved in one-and-a-half training days. It would also be possible to conduct this type of team-building session by taking out one afternoon a week over a period of time, such as three afternoons in one week, or one afternoon for three weeks. Our experience indicates that the time spent in one block allows for more impact to occur. Each time a group meets, a certain amount of "settling-in" time occurs, which is minimized if the sessions are held at one time.

Location.   Off-site conferences are often preferred, since it reduces the possibility of interruptions, phone calls, people going back to the office, etc. On-site programs are not undesirable, but the problem of interferences should be faced directly and an agreement reached to not allow disruptive elements to intrude into the sessions.

It is desirable to have a comfortable room where people can sit in a circle, around a table if this is more comfortable, and talk directly to everyone else. A blackboard, easel, and newsprint and magic markers are also useful.

Resource Personnel.   If the ground rules, procedures, overall goals, and design elements are clear, a manager need not be afraid to conduct this type of meeting with no outside assistance. If certain realistic concerns suggest that an outside person would be helpful in facilitating the meeting, this type of resource person could be included. This person may be someone from within the company, but in a different department (such as an OD specialist), or a consultant from outside the company entirely.

Whether or not an outside resource person is used, the whole team-building meeting should be conducted and "managed" by the senior administrator or boss. Team building is management's business; it is a boss building his or her team. It is *not* an exercise called by a staff person in personnel.

PROGRAM DESIGN

Goal.   The goal of a role relationship team-building program is to arrive at that condition in the work unit where all unit members can publicly agree that they:

1. have a clear understanding of the major requirements of their own job;

2. feel that the others at the team-building meeting also clearly understand everyone's position and duties;

3. know what others expect of them in their working relationships;

4. feel that others know what is expected of them in their working relationships.

All agreements in working relationships are met in a spirit of collaboration and a willingness to implement the understandings. Procedures are established which permit future misunderstandings to be handled in a more effective way.

Prework.   This part of the team-building activity can be done prior to coming to the session, or should be done first by each member of the group in private as the team session begins. Each person should write answers to the following questions:

1. What do you feel the organization expects you to do in your job? (This is the formal job description.)

2. What do you actually do in your job? (Describe your actual working activities and point out any discrepancies between the formal job description and your actual job activities.)

3. Identify specific difficulties or concerns you have had in working with other staff members.

4. What do you need to know about other people's jobs that would help you do your work?

5. What do you feel others should know about your job that would help them do their work?

6. What do you need from others in order to do your job the way you would like?

7. What changes in organization structure, assignments, or activities would improve the functioning of the whole unit?

MEETING DESIGN

All meetings of the team-building program should be conducted by the unit manager. If a consultant is present, he or she should be a resource, but should not conduct the sessions.

Goals.   The goals of the team-building meeting should be presented and clarified and discussed. Everyone should agree on the goals or hoped-for outcomes of the sessions.

Ground Rules.   Ground rules for functioning should be developed from the group, written on a sheet of paper, and posted for all to see. Some suggested ground rules follow:

a) Each person should be as candid and open as possible in a spirit of wanting to help improve the team.

b) If a person wants to know how another person feels or what that person thinks on an issue, he or she should ask that person directly. The person asked should give an honest response, even if it is to say, "I don't feel like responding right now."

c) If the meeting becomes unproductive for any person, he or she should express this concern to the group.

d) Each person should have an opportunity to speak on every issue.

e) Decisions made should be agreeable to all persons affected by the decision.

Job Understanding.   Each person should have a chance to read his or her answers to prework questions 1, 2, and 5. After the person reads an answer, all other team members should have a chance to respond in terms of how they have seen that person's job. It is important for each person to hear how others see his or her job, and also what they would like the person to do on the job that would be of benefit to them. Each person should be given ample time to explore personal job responsibilities with others. This could be from thirty minutes to more than an hour for each person.

Each person should next read his or her answers to question 4 and attempt to get answers from the person(s) identified in the question in the total group. An alternative design is to have group members read their answers to question 4 and then divide up into subgroups, so that people can talk with those individuals they mentioned in their responses.

Concerns.   Each person should read his or her answer to question 3. Many of these concerns may have already been covered in the earlier discussions, but any unresolved concerns should be aired at this time.

As much as possible, try to problem solve and not place blame. It is not as important to fix blame on a person as it is to recognize that a problem exists and to work out a solution.

Change. Each person should read his or her answer to question 7. Change suggestions should be discussed by the group and adopted, modified, or rejected. Every person affected by the change should be heard and should agree. All changes should be recorded and distributed to all members following the session.

Conclusion. At the end of the sessions, the whole team-building program should be critiqued. People should respond to the following questions:

a) How have you felt about the team-building meetings?

b) What were the best parts for you?

c) What needed to be changed or improved?

d) Do we need other sessions like this? If so, what should we discuss? When should we meet again?

This type of team-development meeting is one of the easiest to manage and one of the most productive of all design possibilities for improving team effectiveness. Most groups of people slip into areas of ambiguity in their working relationships. Expectations get formed about performances which people do not understand or even know about. The periodic clarification of roles is a useful process for any working group.

One company's executive committee was conducting a role-clarification meeting. The members of the president's management group were outlining their jobs as they saw them, and what they felt they needed from each other in order to carry out their jobs more effectively. When it came to the personnel manager, she turned to the president and said, "One of the actions I need from you is a chance to get together with you a couple of times a year and review my performance and see what things you feel I need to do to improve."

The president asked in surprise, "Why do you need to get together with me?"

Responded the personnel manager, "When I was hired two years ago, it was my understanding that I was to report directly to you."

"Nobody ever cleared that with me," stated the president. "I thought you reported to the executive vice-president."

The personnel manager had been waiting for two years for a chance to get directions and instructions from the person she thought was her direct superior, but that relationship had never been clarified until the role-clarification session. It's almost like having the center on a football team not knowing that he is supposed to hike the ball to the quarterback.

THE TEAM IN CONFLICT

At times it can be observed that the basic problem in a work unit is the prevalence of highly disruptive conflict and hostility. In some departments, feelings of animosity between individuals or between cliques or subgroups have grown to such proportions that people who must work together do not speak to each other at all. Communications are all by memo, even though offices are adjoining. Why do such conflicts occur and how can a work group resolve such differences? Probably the most common "explanation" for understanding conflict is the "theory" of conflicting personalities. When two people do not get along, a commonplace explanation is to say that their personalities clash. Underlying this is a presumption that the personality of one (a complex of attitudes, values, feelings, needs, and experiences) is so different from the personality of the other that they just cannot function compatibly. Since one's personality is so deeply rooted at the adult stage of life, it seems almost impossible to improve the situation.

Expectation Theory of Conflict

A more useful way to understand conflict is to view it as the result of a violation of expectations. Whenever the behavior of one person violates the expectations of another, it can be predicted that negative reactions will result. If agreements are not reached, the continued cycle of violated expectations and the application of negative sanctions can escalate until open expressions of hostility are common and people are trying to hurt or punish the other in various ways rather than trying to work cooperatively.

One R & D department in a large corporation was split by conflict. There were two warring factions of professionals. For some reason, one group of development researchers felt that the other group got more favors, better facilities, and more rewards than they did. Their expectations were continually being violated. They expected more sharing of research results, more common decision making, more meetings, more equal distribution of rewards. When these expectations were not met, they reacted negatively. These negative responses in turn violated the expectations of the other faction and they reciprocated with their own critical reactions. Before long, the department was filled with unpleasant feelings of hostility.

Expectation theory allows for a greater possibility for dealing with conflict, for it focuses on behavior. If the one faction in the R & D department can begin to identify the behaviors or actions that violate their expectations, perhaps agreements can be negotiated, so that the end result is people rewarding each other rather than applying punishments.

NEGOTIATING AGREEMENTS

In planning a team-building session to deal with conflicts, certain agreements between the clashing parties need to be met: (1) All parties must agree to come together and work on the problems. (2) It helps if people can agree that there are problems, that these problems should be solved, and that all parties have some responsibility to work on the issues. (3) People may find it easier to deal with conflict if they can accept the position that the end result of the team-building session is not to get everyone to "like" each other, but to understand each other and to be able to work together. It is not necessary that everyone form personal friendships, but group members should be able to at least accept each other and meet each other's expectations.

In setting up the team-building session, the disagreeing parties will work best together if they can adopt the position that it is not productive to try and unravel who is at fault or what "caused" the problem; rather, they should accept the fact that differences exist and they need to work out agreeable solutions.

The Start-Stop-Continue Format

When the parties come together in the team-building session, each party builds a list for the other. Each lists the things they would like to see the other group start doing, stop doing, and continue to do if their expectations are to be met and positive results achieved. The parties then share their lists with each other.

Negotiation

With the lists of things that each party wants from the other on display for all to see, a negotiation session ensues. Subgroup A identifies what it wants from subgroup B and vice versa. The two subgroups then agree on what one party will do in return for an equal behavioral alteration on the part of the other. Such agreements can actually be written up. In some cases, signing the agreement increases the commitment to making the change. Such a process puts the formerly warring factions into a problem-solving situation that requires them to try to work out solutions rather than spending their time finding fault, placing blame, or looking for causes of the problems. This negotiation process has been described by Harrison[2] and has been the basis for a company-wide team-development program in the Diamond Shamrock Company.[3]

The design of such a conflict-reducing meeting can vary widely. It may be desirable to precede the session with a presentation of expectation theory and to describe the negative consequences of continued hostility. Another possibility is to have members of each party try to predict what the other group thinks about them and what they think the other group wants from them. These guesses are often surprisingly accurate and may facilitate the coming to agreement.

This design may also be used to negotiate agreements between individuals. If a manager feels the thing most divisive in the team is conflict between two people, the manager can bring these people together and get them into a problem-solving situation where they begin to work out agreements with one another.

---

2   R. Harrison, "Role Negotiations," in W. Burke and H. Hornstein, *The Social Technology of Organization Development* (Washington, D.C.: NTL Learning Resources, 1971).

3   Arthur M. Louis, "They're Striking Some Strange Bargains at Diamond Shamrock," *Fortune*, January 1976, pp. 142–157.

9
OVERCOMING UNHEALTHY AGREEMENT

THE ABILENE PARADOX[1,2]

July Sunday afternoons in Coleman, Texas (population 5,607) are not exactly winter holidays. This one was particularly hot—104 degrees as measured by the Walgreen's Rexall Ex-Lax Temperature Gauge located under the tin awning which covered a rather substantial "screened-in" back porch. In addition, the wind was blowing fine-grained West Texas topsoil through the house. The windows were closed, but dust filtered through what were apparently cavernous but invisible openings in the walls.

"How could dust blow through closed windows and solid walls?" one might ask. Such a question betrays more of the provincialism of the reader than the writer. Anyone who has ever lived in West Texas wouldn't bother to ask. Just let it be said that wind can do a lot of things with topsoil when more than thirty days have passed without rain.

---

1   Much of the material in the section entitled "The Abilene Paradox" was contained in the article by J. Harvey, "Managing Agreement in Organizations: The Abilene Paradox." Reprinted by permission of the publisher from *Organizational Dynamics*, Summer 1974. © 1974.

2   With Jerry Harvey.

But the afternoon was still tolerable—even potentially enjoyable. A water-cooled fan provided adequate relief from the heat as long as one didn't stray too far from it, and we didn't. In addition, there was cold lemonade for sipping. One might have preferred stronger stuff, but Coleman was "dry" in more ways than one; and so were my in-laws, at least until someone got sick. Then a teaspoon or two for medicinal purposes might be legitimately considered. But this particular Sunday no one was ill; and anyway, lemonade seemed to offer the necessary cooling properties we sought.

And finally, there was entertainment. Dominoes. Perfect for the conditions. The game required little more physical exertion than an occasional mumbled comment, "shuffle 'em" and an unhurried movement of the arm to place the spots in the appropriate perspective on the table. It also required somebody to mark the score; but that responsibility was shifted at the conclusion of each hand so the task, though onerous, was in no way physically debilitating. In short, dominoes was diversion, but pleasant diversion.

So, all in all it was an agreeable—even exciting—Sunday afternoon in Coleman; if, to quote a contemporary radio commercial, "You are easily excited." That is, it was until my father-in-law suddenly looked up from the table and said with apparent enthusiasm, "Let's get in the car and go to Abilene and have dinner at the cafeteria."

To put it mildly, his suggestion caught me unprepared. You might even say it woke me up. I began to turn it over in my mind. "Go to Abilene? Fifty-three miles? In this dust storm? We'll have to drive with the lights on even though it's the middle of the afternoon. And the heat. It's bad enough here in front of the fan, but in an unairconditioned 1958 Buick it will be brutal. And eat at the cafeteria? Some cafeterias may be okay, but the one in Abilene conjures up dark memories of the enlisted men's field mess."

But before I could clarify and organize my thoughts even to articulate them, Beth, my wife, chimed in with, "Sounds like a great idea. I would like to go. How about you, Jerry?" Well, since my own preferences were obviously out of step with the rest, I decided not to impede the party's progress and replied with, "Sounds good to me," and added, "I just hope your mother wants to go."

"Of course I want to go," my mother-in-law replied, "I haven't been to Abilene in a long time. What makes you think I wouldn't want to go?"

So into the car and to Abilene we went. My predictions were fulfilled. The heat was brutal. We were coated with a fine layer of West Texas dust which was cemented with perspiration by the time we arrived; and the food at the cafeteria provided first-rate testimonial material for Alka-Seltzer commercials.

Some four hours and 106 miles later we returned to Coleman, Texas, but tired and exhausted. We sat in front of the fan for a long time in silence. Then, both to be sociable and also to break a rather oppressive silence, I said, "It was a great trip, wasn't it?"

No one spoke.

Finally my mother-in-law said, with some slight note of irritation, "Well, to tell the truth, I really didn't enjoy it much and would have rather stayed here. I just went along because the three of you were so enthusiastic about going. I wouldn't have gone if 'you all' hadn't pressured me into it."

I couldn't believe it. "What do you mean 'you all?' " I said, "Don't put me in the 'you all' group. I was delighted to be doing what we were doing. I didn't want to go. I only went to satisfy the rest of you characters. You are the culprits."

Beth looked shocked. "Don't call me a culprit. You and Daddy and Mama were the ones who wanted to go. I just went along to be sociable and to keep you happy. I would have had to be crazy to want to go out in heat like that. You don't think I'm crazy, do you?"

Before I had the opportunity to fall into that obvious trap, her father entered the conversation again with some abruptness. He spoke only one word, but he did it in the quite simple, straightforward vernacular that only a life-long Texan and particularly a Colemanite can approximate. That word was "H-E-L-L."

Since he seldom resorted to profanity, he immediately caught our attention. Then he proceeded to expand on what was already an absolutely clear thought with, "Listen, I never wanted to go to Abilene. I was sort of making conversation. I just thought you might have been bored, and I felt I ought to say something. I didn't want you and Jerry to have a bad time when you visit. You visit so seldom I wanted to be sure you enjoy it. And I knew

Mama would be upset if 'you all' didn't have a good time. Personally, I would have preferred to play another game of dominoes and eaten the leftovers in the icebox."

After the initial outburst of recrimination we all sat back in silence. Here we were, four reasonable sensible people who, on our own volitions, had just taken a one-hundred-six mile trip across a Godforsaken desert in furnace-like temperatures through a cloud-like duststorm to eat unpalatable food at a hole-in-the-wall cafeteria in Abilene, Texas, when none of us had really wanted to go. In fact, to be more accurate, we'd done just the opposite of what we wanted to do. The whole situation seemed paradoxical. It simply didn't make sense.

At least it didn't make sense at that time. But since that fateful summer day in Coleman, I have observed, consulted with, and been a part of more than one organization that has been caught in the same situation. As a result, it has either taken a temporary side-trip, and occasionally, a terminal journey to Abilene when Dallas or Muleshoe or Houston or Tokyo was where it really wanted to go. And for most of those organizations, the destructive consequences of such trips, measured both in terms of human misery and economic loss have been much greater than for the Abilene group.

This story is concerned with a paradox—"The Abilene Paradox." Stated simply, it is as follows: Organizations frequently take actions in contradiction to what they really want to do and therefore defeat the very purposes they are trying to achieve. It also deals with a major corollary of the paradox, which is that *the inability to manage agreement is a major source of organization dysfunction.*

When a group gets lost in such a cloud of unrecognized agreement, it frequently manifests behavior that leads one to mistakenly believe the organization is caught in a dilemma of conflict. For that reason, it takes a different type of team-development problem-solving process involving agreement management to develop new, more functional organizational behaviors.

SYMPTOMS OF THE PROBLEM

Since the surface symptoms (i.e., conflict) of both agreement and disagreement are essentially similar, the first requirement is to be aware of the symptoms of an agreement-management dilemma. Then, on the basis of correctly identifying the symptoms, one can take functional corrective action.

Harvey[3] has identified two sets of symptoms. The first set can most easily be identified by someone outside the system under scrutiny. In effect, being free of the blinding forces of action anxiety, negative fantasies, existential risk and the psychological reversal of risk and certainty, all of which contribute to the Paradox's pernicious influence, he/she can frequently observe symptoms hidden by the dust which is all too familiar to residents of Abilene.

The second set, more subjective in character, can be more easily recognized by persons living within the system.

Symptoms More Easily Observable to Outsiders

Outsiders, including detached laymen or professional consultants, can be relatively sure that the client organization is on a trip to Abilene if they observe the following symptoms:

1. Organization members feel pain, frustration, feelings of impotence or sterility when trying to cope with the problem. In gross terms, there is a lot of apparent conflict.

2. Organization members agree privately, as individuals, as to the nature of the problem facing the organization.

3. Members also agree, privately, as individuals, as to the steps required to cope with the problem.

4. There is a great deal of blaming of others for the conditions they are in.

5. People break into subgroups of trusted friends to share rumors, complaints, fantasies, or strategies relating to the problem or its solution.

6. In collective situations (group meetings, public memos, etc.) members fail to accurately communicate their desires and beliefs to others. In fact, they frequently communicate just the opposite.

---

3   J. Harvey, "Managing Agreement in Organizations: The Abilene Paradox," *Organization Dynamics* (Summer 1974), pp. 63–80.

7. On the basis of such invalid and inaccurate information, members make collective decisions that lead them to take actions contrary to what they personally and collectively want to do.

8. As a result of such counterproductive actions, members experience even greater anger, frustration, irritation, and dissatisfaction with the organization.

9. Members behave differently outside the organization. In other organizations (families, churches, other work units), they are happier, get along better with others, and perform more effectively.

Symptoms More Easily Observable to Insiders

Likewise, some symptoms, stemming primarily from one's subjective experiences within the organization, are more easily identified by persons who are caught up in the problem of mismanaged agreement. For example, if you experience the following feelings within your organization, you may be pretty sure you are lost in a duststorm of agreement and are on a trip to Abilene:

1. You feel pained, frustrated, impotent, sterile, and basically unable to cope when trying to solve a particular organizational problem.

2. You frequently meet with trusted associates over coffee, clandestine lunches or in the privacy of your home or office to discuss the problem, to commiserate with each other, and to plan fantasized solutions which you would attempt "if the conditions were only right." (Fortunately or unfortunately, depending on your point of view, they seldom are.)

3. You blame others, the boss, other divisions, or those "unperceptive people in Unit X" for the dilemma. The boss, in particular, frequently gets an unequal share of the blame and is described with statements such as, "He's out of touch," "She's lost control of the unit," or "He sure as heck isn't as good as Ms. Watson was in dealing with problems like this."

4. In collective meetings where the problem is discussed you are frequently cautious, less than candid, and vague when discussing

your ideas regarding the problem and its solution. Stated differently, you frequently try to determine what others' positions on the issues are without clearly revealing your own.

5. You repeatedly find that the problem-solving actions you take, both individually and collectively, not only fail to solve the problem, but also tend to make it worse.

6. You frequently hold fantasized conversations with yourself of what you might have done—or should have done. "When he said . . ., I wish I would have said. . . ."

7. Finally, you frequently look for ways to escape by taking sick leave, vacation, traveling, or scheduling other "more important meetings" on days when the problem is going to be discussed.

Only when someone in the work unit becomes aware of either or both sets of symptoms does it become possible to design a problem-solving process designed to break out of what is ultimately a self-defeating organizational process.

TEAM DEVELOPMENT
AROUND THE CRISES OF AGREEMENT

Since an essential cause of the hidden-agreement syndrome is that organizational members are afraid to "own up"[4] to their basic concerns, coping with hidden agreement in work groups is especially difficult. That difficulty, in turn, stems from three essential dilemmas: (1) it involves risk and takes skill for an individual to own up to his/her true feelings and beliefs about an issue when other members of the organization have publicly taken different and/or contrary positions; (2) it involves risk and takes skill for others to "own up" to their similar private feelings and beliefs, because of their negative fantasies of the terrible consequences that might occur if they reveal them in an

---

4   The term "own up" has a very precise meaning. Essentially "owning up" is (1) a first-person statement beginning with the word "I" ("I think," "I believe," "I want") in which the individual (2) clearly communicates his/her own ideas and feelings about an issue (3) in a descriptive way, (4) without attributing an idea, a feeling, a belief or a motivation to another.

unequivocal manner; (3) it is very difficult to learn the individual and collective skills required, even if one is willing to accept the risks.[5]

In summary, the possibility that a work unit could exhibit public equanimity, private turmoil, and perform ineffectively is one compelling reason for work groups to hold periodic team review and development sessions when symptoms of the Abilene Paradox are present. Another reason is that the organization might be able to do something constructive about the problem, even though the skills required for success in such a session may not be easy or comfortable to learn.

The manner in which such review and development sessions might be conducted is next discussed.

FORMAT POSSIBILITIES FOR AGREEMENT-MANAGEMENT TEAM-DEVELOPMENT SESSIONS

There are a number of possible formats for taking problem-solving actions. Generally they involve data gathering, theory sharing, and norm setting. Data gathering may be conducted by either insiders or outside consultants. Each approach is described in the following sections.

Data Collection by an Outside Consultant

To surface hidden agreements, it may be useful to have an outside consultant interview people in the organization unit (by an "outside" consultant, we mean someone who is not a part of the blinding, collusive anxiety system which facilitates the hidden-agreement syndrome and who knows the theory and practice of agreement management; in other words, he or she may be a competent professional, friend, or colleague). Based on the theory of agreement management, such a consultant might ask the following questions: (a) What problem does this organizational unit have that you have a hard time accepting, facing, or discussing? (The question assumes the respondent knows the nature of the problem and can state it.) (b) What decisions or actions have recently been taken regarding the problem which you have not really agreed with? (The question helps determine

---

5   See C. Argyris, *Intervention Theory and Method: A Behavioral Science Approach* (Reading, Mass.: Addison-Wesley), 1970; and C. Argyris and D. Schon, *Theory in Practice* (San Francisco: Jossey-Bass), 1974.

whether there are consistent discrepancies between private beliefs and public actions—a key symptom of an agreement-management dilemma.) (c) What actions or decisions do you feel would produce the best results for the organization over the long term? (The question assumes the respondent knows an effective solution to the problem.) (d) What will happen if you don't discuss your concerns, feelings, beliefs, and suggestions with all members of the unit who are involved with the problem? What will happen if you do? (The questions assume fantasized consequences either will help or hinder the individual's making a decision to discuss the issues with others in such a way that the problem might be solved.)

Having gathered the data via interviews, the outside consultant would present a summary of their responses simultaneously to them in a group problem-solving session, designed and "contracted" for, essentially, in the manner described by Beckhard.[6]

Data Collection by Members of the Organization

It is also possible that people from within the organization who are a part of the problem could share data and, by exhibiting such behavior, could encourage others to do the same. In this case, an outside interviewer would not be needed. Again, such data are most effectively shared in a group meeting involving all people key to the problem. In such a meeting, the person who calls it explains his or her desire to "own up" and expresses a desire to know others' beliefs and feelings regarding the issue. A typical statement at the beginning of such a meeting might be as follows: "I have some data I want to share with you. I'm anxious about doing it because I may find I'm the only one who sees the problem this way and I don't like to feel alone. But here it is. I really don't think we are going to succeed on Project X. It's important for me to know how others feel about it though. I would appreciate your letting me know what you think."

Despite the competence and good intentions of the person making such a statement, it is possible that the fear element could be so strong that other members of the organization would be unwilling to surface their true beliefs and feelings; but it is also possible that at least one person would "own up" to his or her concerns and the log

---

6   Beckhard, "The Confrontation Meeting," *Harvard Business Review* (March–April 1967), pp. 149–155.

jam would be broken. Alternatively, in the absence of such "owning" statements, the probability of the problems being solved is reduced.

Sharing the Theory

In addition to data collection and data sharing, an important element of such problem-solving sessions is for all members of the organization to know the theory of agreement management. To accomplish the goal of communicating theory, the story of "The Abilene Paradox," which opens this chapter, could be distributed to all members of the group prior to the problem-solving meeting. Each person could be asked to read the story and be ready to discuss whether he/she had experienced or observed any situations in the past or present, or possibly foresaw some in the future, where the organization is (or would be) in danger of taking a trip to Abilene—i.e., of doing something that no one really wants to do, or of not doing something organization members really want to do. Then, at the problem-solving meeting, each person could be asked to discuss The Abilene Paradox and his/her observations of its actual relevance to the work group.

Since the reactions of authority figures set the parameters of other responses in any type of confrontation meeting, it is helpful if the head of the organization can begin the process and can own up to personal concerns about any trips to Abilene that he or she has observed, participated in, led, or may foresee leading.

Agreements, Decisions, and Actions

Once the work group has discussed the theory of hidden agreements and has shared data about any potential agreements that they may be incorrectly treating as conflicts, it is important to come to valid public agreements about the nature of the "true" conditions that exist, make action plans based on the reality of such truths, and then take steps to reduce the probability of future trips to Abilene.

For example, as valid data to the questions are shared, the issues might be summarized and listed on newsprint by a recorder. Then, on the basis of the data so collected and recorded, the work group could discover those hidden agreements (or real disagreements) both about the organization's basic problems and the solutions that might solve them. To "formalize" the process and to facilitate specific actions, they might also formulate a summary statement that captures the essence of their agreements. For example, if they were to discover a hidden agreement that everyone, including the boss, agreed that the regular staff meetings were poorly planned and a waste of time, they might produce the following summary of their agreement: Our weekly staff meetings are not planned well and do not have a clear enough purpose to make them worthwhile.

As each area of potential agreement is collectively owned up to, the group could continue the discussion until it reaches a valid agreement in the form of a written summary statement about the nature of the problem.

Once there is agreement about the problems, the next step is to come to a decision in writing about new courses of action that would help to resolve these dilemmas. These may take the form of new policies, programs, or activities. For example, if organization members surface the hidden agreement that staff meetings are a waste of time, they might "formalize" the following actions in a problem-solving statement: In the future, no staff meeting will be held unless staff agrees on the agenda and a special committee appointed by the total staff plans the meeting to increase the probability of its success.

PREVENTING FUTURE TRIPS TO ABILENE

Once the immediate problem of specific hidden agreements has been faced, the next step for the group is to establish a process that will reduce the probability that similar problems will occur in the future.

Underlying the whole problem of collective trips to Abilene is fear. Fear, in turn, is a reflection of organization climate, and is both affected by and expressed through negative fantasies. For instance, the climate may be expressed by the fear subordinates express about one powerful person and the manner in which people figuratively tremble because of the fantasies they have about the consequences of disagreeing with that person. Or it may be expressed by fantasized fears of a nonspecific group, such as "top management." Such fantasized fears can both contribute to and also reinforce a general dysfunctional organizational climate, maintained by myths, rumors, and incidents grounded in fact and in fancy.

In addressing this question, the team may arrive at a number of possible procedures that may prove helpful. Some typical procedures suggested by organization members are these:

1. Appoint an organization ombudsman who, in one capacity, functions as a clearing house for all private matters of concern.

2. Periodically invite an external consultant in to interview people about unspoken concerns.

3. Hold regular team-building meetings following the problem-solving format described in earlier chapters.

4. Form an employee panel whose primary function is to talk with others in order to surface potentially controversial concerns and send them in writing to all members of the organization involved in the problem.

5. Make available a form that anyone can fill out anonymously to describe concerns he or she feels personally, but is afraid to share publicly. If more than one person describes the same concern, a meeting is held among the affected parties to discuss the issue or concern.

Although many organizations try such measures, we find that, by themselves, they are effective in the short run but ineffective over the long haul. Their ineffectiveness stems from the fact that, in each of the five procedures, only a minority of the organization—the ombudsman, the internal consultant, and the panel members—have to be both competent and willing to take risks. In fact, one could argue that others in the organization might become more incompetent and irresponsible as a result of having such "crutches" available. ("No need in my saying anything—I'll just let the ombudsman or the employee panel handle it.")

For that reason we prefer an approach where all members learn the extremely difficult skills of owning up, openness, and experimentation, all of which facilitate a climate that fosters individuality (rather than conformity), concern (rather than antagonism), and trust (rather than distrust).

In short, if the problem of hidden organization agreement is to be truly solved, the question to be addressed is this: What skills can organization members learn individually and collectively which will allow them to rely at all times, on the validity of what other members say?

If everyone in the organization can learn such skills, then the responsibility for both the defeats and victories in the area of organization decision making can be honestly and productively shared.

10
REVITALIZING THE COMPLACENT TEAM

PROBLEMS ON A NEW JOB

When Scott Roberts, a new MBA, accepted a position in a medium-sized foods company, he was excited about the prospects of his first major job. He hoped to put to use all of his training and he had some ideas he felt were good which he wanted to share with others in the organization. It didn't take Scott long to learn that people didn't seem to want his bright ideas. After nine months, Scott was convinced that the only people who got ahead in the organization were those who kept their mouths shut, did what they were told, and constantly affirmed their loyalty to the company. Staff meetings were always very pleasant. People went along with whatever the person in charge recommended. Every meeting was conducted the same way—even the agenda items were almost always the same.

People seemed to like their jobs and the company. Most of the personnel had been with the company for more than fifteen years and seemed to be satisfied to continue in the same pattern until retirement. Scott's attempts to raise questions and put in some new suggestions were met with an indulgent smile from his boss who told him that they "liked the 'fire' in the new people, to keep the ideas coming, and they would take his suggestions under advisement." Scott heard no more about them.

When Scott expressed concerns about his job to his wife she

wanted to know what was wrong with the company. Scott had a hard time putting his finger on anything concrete. People treated him well, his work went along smoothly, the future seemed secure. Everything was "just fine" and that was the rub. Scott knew he wanted more out of his work. He needed more challenge, greater stimulation, more exchange, and a chance to match wits with other people. Scott could not help feeling that this company could not hold its own over the long haul against competitors who were aggressively looking at the conditions of the market and coming up with new products that were capturing the attention of the buying public. Scott began seriously to reevaluate his future and his fit with the current company.

A company like the one Scott belongs to could benefit from a program designed to look at its own complacency and lack of innovation and aggressive action concerning the present and future. Teams in this organization are like the baseball team that has become "fat and happy." They may win for awhile longer, but the teams that are hungrier, with more desire, more energy, and more thrust are going to emerge and begin to move ahead. There are many conditions that threaten the effectiveness of a working team, and the lack of imagination and creativity is an eroding spirit that can be met and managed with the right kind of action.

The original team-development designs were created primarily to help deal with issues centered mostly around matters of conflict, disruption, ineffective methods, unclear assignments or expectations, and leadership problems. These generally are areas where something needs to be repaired or a problem solved. However, some organizations or units find that the issue is not a matter of an unsolved problem or a case of disruption, but a situation where people have drifted into a common, routine, standard, accepted way of "doing business." If this kind of team were to be "developed" to improve its effectiveness, the thrust would be in the direction of stimulating greater creativity, more innovation in finding new products or services, more imaginative programs, and new ways to work, thus developing a more zestful, stimulating climate.

DIAGNOSIS

If the following conditions appear, it may be useful for the work unit to consider a team-development program with the goal of stimulating greater imagination and creativity.

1. The same people seem to be doing the same things the same ways year after year, even though other conditions have changed.
2. Products or service levels have stayed constant for some years, although similar units in other organizations have improved.
3. New people often transfer out or quit because the atmosphere is just not challenging enough.
4. The area of greatest pride among workers is their devotion and loyalty to the organization.
5. There seems to be a fear or resistance to risk-taking behavior or trying out something new.
6. The rewards in the organization go to the people who do the solid, standard job. Few rewards go to the person who initiates a new method or product.

A work unit with several of the above conditions might be one where people trust and respect each other and feel good about their manager, where conflicts and disruptions are minimal, and where serious employee or work problems seldom emerge. One might feel that such a unit would be "ideal" and would have no need for a development program. However, if it is seen that external conditions have changed, new demands are present, the old methods are not keeping pace, and young progressive people are choosing other organizations, then perhaps a revitalizing team-development program is appropriate.

Steiner[1] has identified the following as some of the characteristics of a creative organization:

1. includes marginal, unusual types of people;
2. has open channels of communication;
3. encourages contacts with outside sources;
4. experiments with new ideas rather than prejudging on "rational" grounds—everything gets a chance;
5. not run as a "tight ship";
6. employees have fun;

---

1   Gary Steiner, *The Creative Organization* (Chicago: University of Chicago Press, 1965).

7. rewards go to people with ideas;

8. ideas evaluated on their merits, not according to the status of the originator;

9. new, ad hoc approaches are allowed to emerge;

10. risk-taking ethos—tolerates and expects taking chances.

Table 10.1   Encouraging Creativity through Management and Organization*

This scale will help you see to what extent the type of management and the organizational conditions support and encourage creative effort.

1. My ideas or suggestions never get a fair hearing.   1 2 3 4 5 6 7   My ideas or suggestions get a fair hearing.

2. I feel like my boss is not interested in my ideas.   1 2 3 4 5 6 7   I feel like my boss is very interested in my ideas.

3. I receive no encouragement to innovate on my job.   1 2 3 4 5 6 7   I am encouraged to innovate on my job.

4. There is no reward for innovating or improving things on my job.   1 2 3 4 5 6 7   I am rewarded for innovating and improving on my job.

5. There is no encouragement for diverse opinions among subordinates.   1 2 3 4 5 6 7   There is encouragement of diversity of opinion among subordinates.

6. I'm very reluctant to tell the boss about mistakes I make.   1 2 3 4 5 6 7   I feel comfortable enough with my boss to tell about mistakes I make.

7. I'm not given enough responsibility to do my job right.   1 2 3 4 5 6 7   I am given enough responsibility to do my job right.

8. To really suceed in this organization, one needs to be a friend or a relative of the boss.   1 2 3 4 5 6 7   There is no favoritism in the organization.

9. There are other jobs in this organization that I would prefer to have.   1 2 3 4 5 6 7   I have the job in this organization that I think I do best.

10. They keep close watch over me too much of the time.

1 2 3 4 5 6 7

They trust me to do my job without always checking on me.

11. They would not let me try other jobs in the organization.

1 2 3 4 5 6 7

I could try other kinds of jobs in the organization if I wanted to.

12. The management is made very uptight by confusion, disorder, and chaos.

1 2 3 4 5 6 7

The management deals easily with confusion, disorder and chaos.

13. There is a low standard of excellence on the job.

1 2 3 4 5 6 7

There is a high standard of excellence on the job.

14. My boss is not open to receive my opinion of how he/she might improve his/her own performance on the job

1 2 3 4 5 6 7

My boss is very open to suggestions on how he/she might improve his/her own performance

15. My boss has a very low standard for judging his/her own performance.

1 2 3 4 5 6 7

My boss has a very high standard of excellence for judging his/her own performance.

16. I am not asked for suggestions on how to improve service to the customers.

1 2 3 4 5 6 7

The management actively solicits my suggestions and ideas on how to improve service to the customers.

17. My boss shows no enthusiasm for the work we are engaged in.

1 2 3 4 5 6 7

My boss exhibits lots of enthusiasm for the work we are engaged in.

18. Mistakes get you in trouble; they aren't to learn from.

1 2 3 4 5 6 7

Around here mistakes are to learn from and not to penalize you.

19. Someone else dictates how much I should accomplish on my job.

1 2 3 4 5 6 7

I'm allowed to set my own goals for my job.

20. The organization has too many rules and regulations for me.

1 2 3 4 5 6 7

The organization has adequate rules and regulations for me.

*By Philip B. Daniels and William G. Dyer.

The scale presented in Table 10.1 may help you diagnose the level of creativity allowed on the job. It should be recognized that at least two problems in creativity might be identified:

1. All people in the organization or unit may be generally satisfied with what an outside observer might assess as a routine, safe, uncreative climate.

2. Some members of the unit may desire greater support for innovation and change, but other parts of the system repress or deny this.

Before any team-development activity would occur, someone with influence would have to recognize the above conditions existing in the work unit as unproductive, and would have to move for some type of change.

DESIGN ELEMENTS

Data Gathering

Since a team moving along in a "standard" manner may not feel a need for more innovation, there needs to be some process for showing unit members that the usual ways of doing things are not enough and that change, creativity, and innovation will be encouraged. This might be done by any of the following:

1. Gather comparative data showing the performance of this unit compared to other, more innovative, similar groups.

2. If the unit is a pocket of conservatism, comments gathered from other units who are able to see the conditions more clearly might be presented, so that unit members can see their image in the eyes of others.

3. Interviews with unit members may reveal that some are aware of the situation, even though they find it comfortable and satisfying.

4. Management may need to give unit members an honest appraisal of the conditions they see existing.

If the unit tends to discourage creativity to the distress of some members, such conditions can be surfaced by interviews, instruments such as found on Table 10.1, a problem census, or the observations of a process consultant.

For this type of development program, an initial data-gathering phase to surface the need and the reasons for initiating the program is a necessary first step.

Data Sharing and Diagnosis

In this phase, unit members are presented with a summary of the data that have been collected. Group members are then asked to look at the data and to discuss the reasons why such conditions exist, what could be changed, and to agree on some new goals for improvement.

Action Planning

In this phase, actions to be taken can be planned by the whole unit, subgroups with assignments, or a task force with the charge to review the creativity level of the unit and to come up with recommendations for change.

Since the area of creative action may be unfamiliar to the team members, they may need to be supplied with some possible actions that could be taken to stimulate innovation in their work unit, as follows:

a) Conduct seminars on creative thinking.

b) Establish a reward-bonus incentive program for new, productive ideas.

c) Give people some free time for individual or group creative problem solving.

d) Devise a new form of staff meetings which will let people free-wheel, brainstorm, or flow easily with new ideas.

e) Form new or unusual short-term groupings to allow people to cross-fertilize their thinking.

f) Have a laboratory, work shop, or "think tank" with necessary materials for tinkering, thinking, and planning.

g) Conduct performance reviews that support and encourage one's creative efforts, ideas, and actions.

h) Implement a policy that reduces fear of making a mistake if one tries something different.

i) Keep people openly informed about the problems in the organization that need solving.

j) Have a reward and recognition system for the creative person.

k) Ask an outside person to observe current organization functioning to assess creative output and suggest ways of improving innovation.

l) Have a team-development session with the special focus of improving the creative atmosphere and output of the department or unit.

m) Rotate people into different positions or parts of the organization, so there is a new mixture of people working on old problems.

n) Organize a job enrichment session where people devise ways of enriching their own jobs.

The group or groups doing the action planning should consider these and any other alternatives before putting them together into a plan of action.

Creative Exercises in Planning

One possible exercise at a group meeting would be to introduce some new, creative ways of planning that have not been tried before.

1. Have a brainstorming session. See how many different suggestions can be produced by stimulating creativity in the work unit.

2. Have the group spend time looking at possible new products, new services, or new ways of doing work.

3. Give people time to discuss a new idea or approach they may have thought of.

4. It may be possible to engage in some group creativity training. With resource help, look at the elements of individual and group creativity and spend a day in practicing such creativity-developing

activities as: (a) brainstorming, (b) developing analogies, (c) seeing parallels and symbols, and (d) exercises on group problem solving.

The team that is bogged down in complacency, or that fails to use its creative talent effectively, is in danger of falling behind its more creative competition at an increasing rate. Team development for such groups should be centered on breaking these units out of familiar ruts and creating conditions for expanded innovation. This means building in organizational supports for stimulating more creative effort, and also providing some experience in new ways to solve problems and perhaps some training in the creative process.

Increasingly, those who analyze organizations are finding that the underlying cause of much low-level output and dissatisfaction among workers is not the authoritarian boss, but the passive boss and the complacent work group. As we continue to graduate more students with graduate degrees and specialized training at the baccalaureate level, these bright, well-trained young people are going to demand work settings that offer challenge, stimulation, and a chance to use their creativity on the job.

11
REDUCING INTER-TEAM CONFLICT

Thus far this volume has concerned itself with designs and methods for increasing the team effectiveness *within* a work unit. It is often the case that a major organizational problem is the lack of teamwork between units, not inside a unit. In fact, units of organizations that become too cohesive, too self involved and concerned, may be ineffective in their working relationships with other units.

Lawrence and Lorsch in their differentiation-integration model have clearly demonstrated that units of organizations are and should be different. When units have differing tasks, goals, personnel, time constraints, and structures, the functioning of these units is bound to be different. The issue is not how to make all units the same, but how to develop an integrating process which allows these contrasting units to work together. One strategy for bringing greater integration between work units is an inter-team development program.[1]

---

1   The basic theory and method for inter-group processes is found in R. Blake, H. Shepard, and J. Mouton, *Managing Intergroup Conflict in Industry* (Houston: Gulf Publishing Co., 1954). For other discussions on inter-group–building strategies see: J.K. Fordyce and R. Weil, *Managing with People* (Reading, Mass.: Addison-Wesley, 1971), pp. 123–130; R. Beckhard, *Organization Development: Strategies and Models* (Reading, Mass.: Addison-Wesley, 1969); E.H. Schein, *Organizational Psychology* (Englewood Cliffs, N.J.: Prentice-Hall, 1965), Chapter 5.

PROBLEM DIAGNOSIS

An inter-team development program may be considered as a possible action when two or more teams that must collaborate for each to achieve its own unit's objectives experience one or more of the following conditions:

1. Unit members avoid or withdraw from interactions with people from the other unit when they should be spending more working time together.

2. The mutual product or end result desired by both units is delayed, diminished, blocked, or altered to the dissatisfaction of one or both parties.

3. Needed services between units are not asked for.

4. Services between units are not performed to the satisfaction of those in the units.

5. Feelings of resentment or antagonism occur as a result of unit interactions.

6. People feel frustrated, rejected, or misunderstood by those in the other unit with whom they must work.

7. More time is spent in either avoiding or circumventing interaction with the other unit, or internally complaining about the other unit, than in working through mutual problems.

DESIGN STRATEGIES

If at least one of the managers in the dysfunctional unit interaction diagnoses the situation accurately and is willing to contact the other unit manager, an inter-unit team-development program may be proposed. It is necessary to get agreement of *both* units to move the program ahead.

The goal of the program is to develop a problem-solving process that will reduce the existing dysfunctional interaction and allow future problems to be solved more effectively before a breakdown in unit interaction occurs. Following are possible design strategies for planning and conducting the proposed program.

In preparation, members of both units should have the purpose and format of the program explained to them. This could be done by the manager involved or in conjunction with an outside facilitator. Agreements to participate should be achieved in both units.

Plans should be made for a block of time to get the appropriate people from both units to work on the interface problems. If the two units are small, it may be possible to involve all unit personnel. If units are larger, it may be necessary to have representatives work through the problem areas.

Design A

a) Appropriate members from Units X and Y meet to work out a more functional method of operating. Members are introduced and the plan, purpose, and schedule of the program are reviewed.

b) Establish ground rules. The essential ground rules are that people should agree to adopt a problem-solving stance. The issue is to work out a solution, not to accuse or fix blame. Members should agree to look at the behavior of their own group members and identify times when their own members are trying to accuse, fix blame, or defend a position rather than solve the problem.

c) Unit members *in their own groups* begin work on the following task: On sheets of newsprint, answer the following.

1. What actions does the other unit engage in that create problems for us? List.

2. What actions do we engage in that we think may create problems for them? List.

3. What recommendations would we make to improve the situation?

d) Each unit brings its sheets of paper and gives them to the other unit to review.

e) Time is spent for each unit to review the work of the other unit and to ask questions for clarification. Agreements and disparities in the two lists are noted.

f) Members of the two units are now put into *mixed teams* composed of an equal number of members from both units. The first task is for each team to review the lists and come up with an agreed-on list of the major problems or obstacles that keep the two units from functioning together effectively.

Each mixed team presents its list of problems to the total group and the results are tabulated. The major agreed-on problems are then identified and listed.

g) Members return to the mixed teams. Each mixed team is given one of the problems identified to work out a recommended solution. This should include: what the problem is; what actions should be taken; who should be responsible for what actions; what the time schedule is; how we plan to keep the problem from occurring again.

h) Mixed teams bring their solutions back to the total group for review and agreement, particularly from those who must implement the actions.

Design B

This design is similar to A. However, instead of the two teams doing their work alone and then presenting the sheets to the other, each unit discusses its issues *in front of* the other group. This is a "fishbowl" design.

a) Group X sits together in a circle. Group Y sits outside and observes and listens. Group X members discuss the three questions listed in part c of Design A. A recorder writes down the points of the discussion.

b) Group Y now moves into the center circle. Group X observes and listens.

c) Following the fishbowl, mixed teams are formed and they perform the same tasks as in Design A.

Design C

A variation on designs A and B is to have the units discuss different questions. The designs are the same—only the questions are different.

1. How do we see the other unit? What is our image of them?

2. How do we think the other unit sees us? What is their image of us?

3. Why do we see them the way we do?

4. Why do we think they see us as we think they do?

5. What would have to change so we would have a more positive image and interaction with each other?

Design D

a) An outside facilitator interviews members of both units privately prior to the team-development session. He or she tries to identify the problems between the units, the source of the problems, and people's recommended solutions.

b) At the inter-team meeting, the facilitator summarizes the results of these interviews. The summaries are printed or posted for all to see.

c) Mixed teams from both units review the summary findings and list the major areas they feel need to be resolved. Major areas are agreed on by the total group.

d) Mixed teams engage in coming up with recommended solutions to the problem assigned to them.

Design E

This design involves selecting a mixed task force composed of members from both units. The job of the task force is to review the interface problems and then recommend solutions to the problems for both groups to consider and agree on.

a) Representatives of the task force are selected in the following manner. Team X lists *all* of its group members who the group feels could adequately represent them on the task force. This list is given to Team Y. Team Y then selects the three or four members from Team X they feel would best represent their interests. Both units engage in this listing and selecting process. The result is a mixed task force composed of members agreeable to both units.

b) The task force may work in many ways. They may wish to interview people from the other units. They may wish to invite a facilitator to work with them. Whatever their working style, they are asked to come up with: the major conditions blocking inter-team effectiveness; what actions should be taken; who should be responsible for what actions; time frame; how we can prevent these problems from occurring again or what method we will use for solving other problems that may arise.

DISCUSSION

Since a variety of inter-team–building models are available, what determines which model would be most appropriate? One factor to consider is the confidence and competence of the unit managers to conduct such a program alone, without the help of an outside facilitator. If they choose to conduct the session alone, it would be wise to select an alternative that is simple, easy to communicate to others, with minimal chance for slippage in the implementation. Design E, the selection of an inter-team task force, is the most traditional way to work on inter-team problems and is probably the easiest alternative to implement without help. It is also the design that has the least involvement of all the members of the two groups and may have the least impact, at least initially.

Design A probably is the most straightforward problem-solving format with the least possibility of surfacing conflicts and issues that could erupt into an unproductive rehash of old grievances. The fishbowl design may create reactions to individuals as they are observed that may be difficult to handle without a trained facilitator, and approaching the issue via an examination of mutual images (Design C) may also give rise to feelings and reactions that may be disruptive to one not used to handling such concerns.

CONCLUSIONS

Inter-group problems open up the issue about the unit to which one has commitment and what is the ultimate "team." In modern organizations, it is not enough to build intense loyalty into the work unit or department, particularly at the expense of the larger total organization. Unless people in different departments that must collaborate can see the larger picture and understand that the team is more than the small group, inter-group conflicts can and do emerge. Team-building sessions *between* units can be conducted before problems occur to cement relationships and establish working guidelines. Certainly it is important to get work units together and iron out difficulties when inter-group problems occur. Single-unit loyalty can be detrimental to achieving total-organization goals.

PART 5
PROBLEMS AND PROSPECTS

12
SPECIAL PROBLEMS IN TEAM BUILDING

When a team-development effort is first introduced into an organization, one can anticipate a series of common concerns, areas of resistance, and blocks to moving ahead. People will hesitate to start a new
program for many reasons. Some fear it will have negative consequences for them. Others ask: Is the time taken worth the effort
expended and the results obtained? Is this just another fad of management that will play itself out, only to be replaced by a new contri-
vance? Rumors may have been circulated about team building having
negative effects. Or, people may simply feel awkward and unskilled in
the new activity. These are common problems that generally can be
handled by holding preliminary meetings to explain in detail the
purpose and format of the program and to allow people to express
concerns and deal with feelings of resistance.

However, certain special problems or issues may still present a
serious roadblock to even starting a team-development program.
These should be discussed here so that they can be handled prior to
starting the program or built into the design; in this way, the concern
can be *appropriately* dealt with during the program.

WHEN THE BOSS IS THE MAJOR PROBLEM
It is not infrequent to find that the biggest problem that interferes with
a working unit functioning effectively as a team is the boss or

manager. If the boss is unaware of this, the situation becomes especially difficult, since unit members are often unwilling to confront the boss with the disruptive consequences of his or her own managerial behavior. If this issue is avoided during the team-building session, all other actions will probably be seen as mere window dressing, for the main issue has been carefully sidestepped. How do you get at the problem manager? He or she may exhibit a streak of authoritarianism, or may be seen as untrustworthy, manipulative, incompetent, punitive, vindictive, withdrawn or isolated, timid and afraid to take action, outdated in management approach, too busy, or any one of a number of other things. Since the boss is the problem center, people may feel that any team-building effort is useless unless the boss makes some changes—yet they are often reluctant to raise the issue with the boss for fear of negative consequences. It may also be that they are fond of their boss, recognize these weak spots, and are afraid to point them out for fear it will "hurt" the boss in some way or disrupt their good boss-subordinate relationship.

Certain kinds of actions are available to focus in on the problem boss and minimize the risk to the rest of the group. Most of these actions involve helping the manager get some insight into his or her impact on others—the possible negative effects he or she is having—*prior* to beginning the team-building program. With this understanding, the manager can take the initiative in examining his or her role in a team-development effort. If the manager can initiate this role analysis in the unit, it is considerably easier for subordinates or co-workers to respond, without fear of unpleasant consequences.

Laboratory Training

Through the years, one of the best methods for preparing a manager to begin a program of planned change in his or her own organization has been for the manager to attend a laboratory program centered on experience-based learning. Argyris[1] has earlier described the functions of a T-group for executives and the literature abounds in detailed descriptions of laboratory education.[2] A number of reputable orga-

---

1   C. Argyris, "T-Groups for Organizational Effectiveness," *Harvard Business Review* **42**, no. 2 (March–April 1964): p. 60–74.

2   See L.P. Bradford, J.R. Gibb, K.O. Benne, *T-Group Theory and Laboratory Method* (New York: Wiley, 1964); and E. Schein and W. Bennis, *Personal and Organizational Change Through Group Methods* (New York: Wiley, 1965).

nizations conduct laboratory programs for managers—National Training Laboratories, Behavioral Science Resources, UCLA, University Associates, Scientific Methods, AMA, plus many more universities and training and consulting organizations.

A primary objective in any laboratory program is to help the participating managers clearly look at their own behavior and see some of their blind spots, begin to understand the utility of interpersonal feedback and group problem solving, and to start them thinking on how they might begin to improve their actions back home. A good laboratory program is an excellent way to prepare the "problem" manager to start a team-development program. How do you get a manager to go to the training program? There's the rub. If a manager doesn't feel he or she needs the program or is too threatened to participate, it is difficult to force the issue.

Some companies regularly have their managers attend a laboratory program as a basic experience for everyone, assuming that the problem manager will be stimulated enough to follow up with a back-home program provided the company is encouraging ongoing team development. Laboratory training without some systematic follow-up activity in the back-home organization tends to have only sporadic long-run benefits to the organization.

A variety of other methods have been used to suggest to a "problem" manager that laboratory or some other training would be a helpful prelude to some intensive development work with the total unit. Sometimes the role of the personnel manager is to pick up data from people in a manager's unit about the manager's need for additional training. The personnel manager may then make recommendations to the manager. In-company surveys may point out the need for some managers to have additional exposure to training methods designed to help them see themselves more clearly. The function of an outside consultant may be to recommend needed training. Third-party facilitators (another manager, a higher-level manager, a friend) may have data about a manager's performance which will prompt them to suggest further training. And, it has even been known for a group of subordinates to suggest to their boss that he might benefit from a week in a T-group.

Management Profiling

A newer method for preparing a manager for starting a team-building effort is management profiling. This procedure involves gathering data via instruments about the manager from his or her subordinates, peers, and superior. The data is then summarized and presented to the manager for analysis. These data, if properly and honestly completed, will help the manager see—in private—the areas of concern, and can get the manager psychologically prepared to deal with his or her role in the unit.

Organizations offering profiling procedures, with instruments and methods for helping a manager get more insight, include Behavioral Science Resources, Telometrics, Scientific Methods, and 3-D, among others. Usually in this process, a person from outside the manager's unit (a personnel person from the company or an outside consultant) is in charge of administering the instruments, preparing the summary, feeding the data back to the manager, and helping the manager plan the next step, which is often some form of feedback of results to the total work group, which then begins a team-building program.

Again, the problem is to induce the manager to engage in a profiling procedure. Methods similar to those described above for stimulating attendance at a laboratory are commonly used.

Interviewing or Surveys

Many organizations will have available one or two common data-gathering procedures designed to uncover problems in the organization. One is to have an outsider come in and interview people about conditions in the work unit, a procedure that could easily reveal some problem with the boss. The advantage of this process is that it allows the boss to review the data and prepare to begin a program, for without the information he or she may not recognize a need or be prepared to move ahead. An organization survey instead of personal interviews is another method with similar results.

The Use of an Honest Observer

Any manager might well assume that certain parts of his or her management style create problems for others. To make sure that these areas are confronted in a team-building session, the manager may wish to invite in a subordinate, co-worker, or a forthright observer and ask, in confidence, what that person sees as the areas that the manager needs to examine in helping build a better working relationship with the work group.

Dealing with the Problem-Manager Issue

Assuming that the manager has some difficulties with the staff and that they are reluctant to raise the issue out of fear, mistrust, or over-concern, and assuming that the manager has taken one of the above steps and now wants to deal directly with the issue of personal effectiveness, how can this be handled? Probably the least threatening process is for the manager to ask—and the subordinates to give.

If a manager asks, "What about my style don't you like or what gives you trouble?" subordinates may feel very uncomfortable replying candidly. However, if the manager asks, "Do you have any suggestions about how I might improve our staff meetings (or our decision making, or our planning, etc.)?" suggestions are likely to be forthcoming. To respond about what one likes or dislikes forces some kind of judgment or evaluation, but the giving of suggestions is more likely to be perceived by the asker and giver as a helpful activity with less implicit threat.

TWO-PARTY CONFLICTS

Sometimes a major disruptive element in a work unit is a problem between two people—two co-workers or the boss and a subordinate. If such is the case, the rest of the team members would like to see the differences resolved, but may feel it inappropriate to deal with the issue in front of the whole group. Should such an issue be raised, it is often more useful for the team if the two members get together privately sometime during the team-building program and work on their differences. Walton[3] has identified the effective use of a third-party facilitator in helping deal with such matters. It is helpful, however, if the persons involved communicate to the rest of the group something of the nature of their resolution, particularly if the group has identified this as a problem that has been affecting the team.

This issue should not be confused with a problem that may concern the manager and the total group, with one person being the spokesman for the whole. In this case, it may be better for the manager and the spokesman to deal with the issue with the others present, with the ground rule that only the spokesman shall participate

---

3   R. Walton, *Interpersonal Peacemaking* (Reading, Mass.: Addison-Wesley, 1969).

in the exchange. A time-out could be called if the spokesman wishes to confer with the others, or if the manager feels it necessary to get more data or authority from his or her boss.

EMERGENT ISSUES

From time to time, new issues or problem areas arise that threaten to disrupt a working unit. Some of the current concerns facing many organizations are the matters of minority-group activities and women's rights.

Sometimes a team will handle the new situation entirely within its own normal group processes. The issue gets raised and the group makes the necessary adjustments to accommodate a new element into its system. If such is the case, there is no need for any special work to pull the unit together for a special team-building meeting around the new issue.

However, if the emergent issue is not handled in the course of normal group operation, it would be wise for the manager to call a special team-development meeting to tackle the new problem area. The format of such a meeting should always be problem focused and centered on actions. If the matter of racism were raised, it would hardly be productive to spend time in making charges and counter charges as to who is or is not racist. The problem-solving stance should be: What actions do we need to take to eliminate any feelings that racism occurs in our team? Then the focus of the group's attention is on planning and action taking—not on name calling or derisive confrontation.

13
WHEN TEAM BUILDING SHOULD NOT BE USED

SHOULD EVERYONE USE TEAM BUILDING?

It seems obvious that all work units are not "teams" in the sense that the people involved must work together to achieve results. How do you determine whether or not this new methodology of team development is appropriate for your situation? In a thoughtful article, Lewis[1] identifies certain basic assumptions which, if not met, would suggest that team building would not be appropriate. He says:

> Team development and a decision to pursue it in an organization rest on a number of critical implicit assumptions. It is worthwhile to identify them, since if one or more of these assumptions do not apply to a particular management group or its situation, undertaking a team development effort may be unnecessary, detrimental, or both.

— Current patterns of communication and interaction among members of a group are inadequate for group and organizational needs.

---

[1]   John W. Lewis, III, "Management Team Development: Will It Work for You?" *Personnel* (July-August 1975).

___ The concept of being (or desiring to be) an integrated team exists in the minds of the executive and managers in the group.

___ Significant face-to-face interaction among members of the group is expected by the executive and/or is required by the needs of the organization.

___ The executive can and will behave differently as a result of the development effort, and team members can and will respond to his new behavior.

___ The organizational tasks assigned to the group require close and frequent coordination laterally among group members in such matters as planning, problem solving, and decision making.

___ The benefits in terms of group effectiveness and member satisfaction to be gained from team development outweigh the costs incurred from altering existing role and social network arrangements to which the group has accommodated.

Lewis also points out that team development must be congruent with the manager's own personal style and philosophy of management as to how to use his or her staff. He says that you should use the team approach only if, as the manager, you find:

1. You are comfortable in sharing organizational leadership and decision making with subordinate managers and prefer to work in an egalitarian atmosphere.

2. A high degree of interdependence exists among functions and managers in order to achieve overall organizational goals.

3. The external environment is highly variable and/or changing rapidly.

4. The organization is young and/or undergoing major change, which results in fluid structure, few operating policies and procedures, and emerging role definitions. The distinction between "line" and "staff" departments is blurred or meaningless.

5. The organization's dominant technologies are relatively new and/or developing rapidly.

6. Broad consultation among your managers as a group on goals, decisions, and problems is necessary on a continuing basis.

7. Members of your management team are (or can become) compatible with each other and are able to create a collaborative rather than competitive working environment.

8. Members of the management team are located close enough to meet frequently and on short notice.

9. You are dependent on the ability and willingness of subordinate managers to resolve critical operating problems directly and in the best interests of the organization as a whole.

10. Formal communication channels are not sufficient for the timely exchange of essential information, views, and decisions among members of the management team.

11. Organizational adaptation requires the frequent use of project management, temporary task forces, and/or ad hoc problem-solving groups to augment conventional organizational structures.

Problems can arise if a manager or an organization-development specialist sees team building as a general activity that all work units should experience. The indiscriminate use of this methodology can have disruptive effects on the unit for whom it is inappropriate; consequently, a generally negative image of team building can emerge, so that those teams that could benefit will shy away from the process.

In light of the agreements presented by Lewis and reviewing the whole issue of team development, before any team building program is started, the following conditions should be assessed:

1. Is the work unit one where collaborative action is essential for good achievement? If work is done primarily on an individual basis or requires only a limited amount of interaction, personal consultation and planning may be more useful than team development.

2. Is the manager familiar with and committed to the idea of team improvement? Often the manager in charge does not understand the long-term nature of a team-building program and is not really willing to invest the necessary time, resources, and energy. He or she may be interested in only a one- or two-day program, with the expectation that all problems will then be solved and business can proceed as usual. Should such be the case, the manager needs a clearer orientation to the nature of the program he or she is buying into.

3. Is there a feeling of "hurt" or a need to see improvement? Team-development programs have limited impact when the initial motivation to begin such a program stems from the push of the training department, or a need to spend training and development funds before they are lost, or because someone has heard about the process and thinks it might be a "good thing for us."

4. Are people in the work unit willing to look at their own unit and engage in problem-solving actions? Where there is low interest in the examination of processes or in honestly critiquing how things are in the work unit, team-building activities are a risk. Low interest can stem from fear, apathy, or cynicism that "nothing ever really happens around here. We start things, but never complete them."

5. Is there enough time and availability of personnel to start such a program? Sometimes there is need and interest for team development, but people are (or feel they are) too busy with work deadlines, projects, or other demands to launch a new program. Before such a program should be started, the key people must be interested and have the time available to be involved.

6. Are the manager and others in the work unit willing to look at their own performance and the work of the unit, willing to give and receive feedback, and honestly interested in making change? Where there is a lack of skill and/or understanding of the processes of team development, people may find that they have begun a program that involves them in actions they didn't bargain for. Team building often requires people to take a hard look at what they are doing. It often means somebody has to make changes. People may get feedback that they'll find disturbing. Being aware of these possibilities in advance and some skill in engaging in change processes is highly desirable before team building begins.

7. Have people already made up their minds what the problems are and what must be done? Team development functions best if there is an openness to data and a willingness to move in the direction the data suggest. If it has already been decided that a certain action must be taken or certain changes made, and if the team-building program is undertaken merely to confirm these moves and make it seem that the people have decided these things for themselves, such actions are usually perceived as manipulative and result in greater resentment, resistance, and cynicism.

SOME CAUTIONS IN TEAM BUILDING

Assuming that the above issues have been confronted and honestly appraised positively, and a team-building program begins, certain cautions or guidelines might well be kept in mind:

1. Team building takes time. You will not see entrenched behaviors and actions turned around early or easily. Action steps must be managed and agreed-on changes must be revised and rewarded regularly to move new behaviors onto a permanent level. One should think of team development as a process that should continue over a period of from one to three years.

2. People in power positions must support changes. Team building as a process will surely not have a long-term impact if people who are in positions of power do not support the solutions to problems suggested by team-development procedures. A manager cannot ask subordinates to spend time and energy wrestling with organization problems and then go about business as usual, ignoring or even blocking the efforts he has asked his own people to produce. Unfortunately, such has been the case in several team-development efforts. One more effective manager took the following stance regarding the actions developed in the team-building sessions. He told his people, "We will set up agreeable terms to review the results of the actions established. Your performance review and the subsequent raises and promotions will be to a large extent contingent on your willingness and ability to implement the actions agreed on." This represents a real commitment on the part of a manager to support the decisions arrived at via the team-building process.

3. Changes need to be built into structure. When a work unit engages in a team-development process, it is trying to solve its own problems and develop a pattern of team effectiveness so that the unit can continue to identify its own problem areas and quickly move to a procedure of diagnosis and problem solving. The solutions developed will be more lasting if they are incorporated into the established structures of the organization. Should a team find it lacks a coordination and integration of roles, a solution that is hammered out in a team-building session may become more permanent if clear job descriptions are developed, coordination procedures adopted, and a review of coordination efforts built into a semiannual review by the manager in

charge. This should help insure a continuation of the action desired, even if there is a turnover of personnel, or a change of focus or demand on the work unit later on.

4. Involvement enhances commitment. There is ample evidence to indicate that people will have greater commitment to decisions, goals, and actions they have participated in developing. Managers who impose team-building activities on others and then force or manipulate desired outcomes without allowing honest involvement of group members run the risk of a long-run failure, even though they went through a team-development activity. People should feel that they are honestly involved and listened to, and that their real ideas and concerns are taken into account.

5. Team development may need to be done more than once. In today's organizations, there is often a great deal of personnel turnover. The composition of a work group can change radically in just a few years. When key people in a department are replaced, the new configuration of personalities and perhaps new assignments and expectations may make another team-development process useful if not mandatory. Agreements made with one set of people may not persist with the change of personnel and the new group may need to go through the whole process again.

14
TEAM DEVELOPMENT:
WHERE DOES IT GO FROM HERE?

Some who read this volume may legitimately raise the question: Isn't team development just another of the current fads in organization and management? We have seen the rise of a variety of programs in the past fifteen years or so—MBO, Motivation-Hygiene, OD, T/A, Theory X & Y, The Grid, T-groups, Gestalt Therapy for Managers, operant conditioning, and on and on. Won't team development wind up like all the rest? Probably! All of the rest (those cited above) have now found their appropriate place in the body of literature, training, and education of new managers. What was once seen as the new cure-all for organization problems (MBO, for example) has now been tested, sifted, and winnowed—the chaff has been discarded and the solid contribution remains. Many organizations that tried to impose a total MBO program on their members and found a mismatch between the program and the readiness of the people may have rejected the notion of a total MBO program, but may have picked up on the idea that individuals and units should set clearer, better goals and should work out plans for achieving them. This is their own MBO program—not exactly like the one originally prescribed, but appropriate for their situation. Thus, MBO did have its impact. New MBA graduates have examined the concept of MBO and are more prepared to deal with the reality of managing for results.

Team building will probably have such a future. It will get built into the management practices of organizations to such a degree that managers will just take it as a matter of fact that one of their responsibilities is to insure cohesion, collaboration, and joint planning and decision making as needed. They will wonder about all the fuss raised in the 1960s and 1970s regarding "team building."

Right now we are still in the transition stage. Many organizations or units of organizations are managed by one-person rule, while the rest of the unit smothers its feelings and talents. Other organizations that should have high collaboration between members are split into factions; conflict, either hidden or open, is the daily experience. And many managers don't know what to do about it. In ten years, most managers will take team building, unit development, organizational integration, or whatever it will be called then as one of the prerequisites of doing the manager's job. There will undoubtedly be less need for outside consultants to assist in the process. Managers will be aware of the variety of methods for gathering data about the state of affairs in their work groups and will quickly identify any problems and raise them for prompt solutions. Hopefully organizations of the future will have effective open feedback systems, so that whenever a problem arises that presents a threat or possibility for disruption, someone with confidence that it will be handled appropriately will immediately raise the issue. In such an open-feedback problem-solving system there will be no need for special team-development meetings; the unit functions as a team every day.

On the other hand, it is quite likely that the organizations of the future will become more flexible, quicker to shift people to meet the new demands of what has been an increasingly rapidly changing society and world (see Toffler's *Future Shock*). If such is the case, people will need to learn to form teams quickly—to establish working relationships that are effective and ground rules that are accepted and viable. Only in this way can they get on with the work at hand without getting bogged down in the misery of ineffective wheel spinning that characterizes so much of the current committee work done in organizations.

Organizations of the future may require that a person belong to several units at the same time and have two, three, or even four bosses. People may shift rapidly from one temporary system to another, and, if such is the case, that organization with managers who know how to build effective teams in a hurry will have a special advantage.

Right now one of the problems of team development in organizations involves the "spread" effect. In trying to change the organization's culture, team building has proven to be a rather slow method in terms of "spreading" the new, more collaborative processes throughout a large organization. It is foolhardy to begin team development at the top of the organization in the hope that managers will spread the process down. This procedure takes so long that by the time the lower levels of the organization experience the impact of team building, the top levels have moved to other matters or the composition of the higher teams has changed and the interlocking spread effect has been lost.

In the organization of the future, certainly new, more innovative methods for introducing team development organizationwide will be available. Already there are experiments in high-spread methods. Some work has been done in training all managers in an organization at once to go immediately into a team-building program—all at the same time. Video and audio tapes have been utilized to expose all teams to the same set of instructions, examples, and training materials. The methodology for quickly spreading team development through the organization is even now in the growing stages.

Team development does not mean managing by committee, where no one is in charge and all actions must be decided by all. A team is a unified, cohesive group of people who have special functions, but each person needs the resources and support of others to get the job done. Team effort will continue as long as humans must rely on others to achieve results.